Easy
Cooking

LA BONNE CUISINE

Easy
Cooking

100 delicious recipes from
Cuisine et Vins de France

whitecap

Contents

Introduction _____ 4

Appetizers & light starters _____ 6

Soups _____ 20

Salads _____ 34

Tarts _____ 48

Gratins _____ 64

Fish & seafood _____ 76

Meat _____ 96

Vegetarian _____ 118

Desserts _____ 142

Index _____ 182

10 steps that make life easier in the kitchen

1   Before you start cooking, organize your kitchen and prepare the ingredients and utensils you will need. This will save you time.

2   Read the recipe all the way through and place everything you need in the way of utensils and ingredients close at hand.

3   Prepare the various ingredients in advance – such as diced onions or shallots, chopped herbs, spices, and the correct amounts of water and butter – and place them in separate bowls on your kitchen worktop.

4   **Keep things simple:** a simple recipe prepared well with good-quality ingredients is better than a sophisticated dish that doesn't live up to expectations. Turn a basic carrot salad into an exotic dish by simply adding orange, cinnamon, and a sprinkling of pomegranate seeds or flaked almonds. A rice pudding with a touch of vanilla will delight any gourmet!

5   Do not add any more than three flavors to the main ingredient of your dish, whether it is meat, grains, legumes, fish, vegetables, or fruit. Too many flavors won't make the dish any tastier, quite the contrary.

6   Use seasonal food products whenever possible. Not only are they tastier, they are also more reasonably priced.

7   Make your life easier by having a permanent stock of some basic products in your kitchen, such as ready-made pastry, frozen herbs, bouillon cubes, and canned tomatoes.

8   **Keep in mind the following tips for seasoning your dishes:** always have some garlic, shallots, or onions at hand. Add any chopped herbs at the end of the cooking process rather than at the beginning so they are still fresh. Make sure you have a nice selection of spices (such as cinnamon, nutmeg, ginger, turmeric, and star anise) for oven-baking fruits. Marinate meat and fish and always use freshly ground pepper.

9   **Make sure you have some good, basic kitchen utensils:** excellent kitchen knives are essential, as are a decent size chopping board; a food processor that can grate vegetables and make pastry; a hand-held blender for preparing soups and sauces; a grater or vegetable slicer; a good-quality casserole dish; and a non-stick frying pan.

10   **Try out these wonderful products, which can transform a dish:** a small bottle of truffle oil will do wonders to a warm potato salad, sautéed chard, root vegetable soup, and scrambled eggs. Top-quality olive oil or walnut oil adds a little extra to carpaccio, crudités, and grilled fish. Sherry, wine, or fruit vinegars enhance vinaigrettes and can also be used to deglaze any meat juices. Different types of pepper are very useful for spicing up a variety of dishes.

Appetizers &
Light Starters

Serves 4

- 20 g (¾ oz) butter
- 20 g (¾ oz) dried breadcrumbs
- 100 g (3½ oz) spicy chorizo
- 100 g (3½ oz) green pitted olives
- 100 g (3½ oz) black pitted olives
- 20 g (¾ oz) cornstarch
- 25 cL (1 cup) cold whole milk
- 2 whole eggs & 2 egg yolks
- 25 cL (1 cup) table cream (18%)
  or light cream (10%)
- salt
- pepper

Chorizo & olive clafouti

Convivial

Preparation: 30 min – Cooking time: 35 min

Preheat the oven to 180°C (350ºF) (th. 6). Butter a 25-cm (10 inch) diameter cake pan and sprinkle the breadcrumbs over the butter, including the edges.

Peel the skin off the chorizo and cut the sausage into thin, round slices. Cut the olives into round slices. Place the chorizo slices on the bottom of the cake pan and then add the slices of olive.

In a Bowl, dillute the cornstarch in the cold milk. In another bowl, beat the eggs, the yolks, and the light cream with a hand whisk. Add the diluted cornstarch and whisk again until the mixture is smooth.

Season with salt and pepper. Pour the mixture over the chorizo and olives and place the cake pan in the oven for about 35 minutes.

Remove the clafouti from the oven. Once it has cooled, cut it into large cubes. Skewer the cubes with wooden cocktail sticks and serve as an appetizer.

Suggested wine pairing: a white Côtes de Provence.

Chorizo: a very versatile ingredient

This famous Spanish specialty, made from lean meat and pork fat, is flavored with garlic, salt, oregano, spices, and chili pepper. The red pepper, a sort of paprika that is used in traditional Spanish cuisine, is known as pimenton. It colors the sausage and, depending on the amount, makes the chorizo either spicy or mild.

Diced or sliced, chorizo adds color and flavor to the most basic dishes:

• Celeriac, cauliflower, zucchini, tomato, or butternut squash soup.

• Pan-fried or oven-baked white fish fillets, such as cod or sablefish.

• Monkfish tail, either oven-baked or on skewers.

• Eggs: scrambled, coddled, or in an omelet.

• Legumes, such as lentils, dried beans, or chickpeas.

• Cooked rice with small cubes of peppers and tomatoes.

• Tomato sauce for a pizza or pasta.

• A variety of salads, including rice, bulgur, quinoa, or endive.

Zucchini, chicken & Parmesan salad

Light

Preparation: 20 min – Cooking time: 10 min

Serves 4

- 2 chicken fillets
- 4 dessert spoons (2¾ Tbsp) olive oil
- 2 dessert spoons (1¼ Tbsp) balsamic vinegar
- 1 slice of Parmesan (about 50 g / 1¾ oz)
- 4 small zucchinis
- 2 dessert spoons (1¼ Tbsp) chopped cilantro
- salt • pepper

Cut the chicken into strips. Heat a spoonful of oil in a frying pan and sear the chicken over high heat for 5 minutes, while turning regularly to avoid over browning. Deglaze with 1 dessert spoon (2 tsp) of balsamic vinegar. Leave to cool.

Meanwhile, use a vegetable peeler to slice the Parmesan into shavings. Wash and dry the zucchini then grate it lengthwise (using the vegetable slicing slot of the grater) to obtain long, spaghetti-like strands. Blanch the zucchini for 2 minutes in salted, boiling water before immersing it in ice-cold water.

Use a fork to combine the salt, pepper, remaining vinegar, and oil in a mixing bowl. Stir in the zucchini strands, the chicken, and cilantro. Sprinkle the salad with the Parmesan shavings and serve.

Suggested wine pairing: a Coteaux Varois (a Provence red).

Serves 4

- 2 leeks (white parts only)
- 200 g (7 oz) white button mushrooms
- juice of ½ a lemon
- 1 bunch flat-leaf parsley
- 2 dessert spoons (1¼ Tbsp) olive oil
- salt
- 4 round sheets of phyllo pastry
- 4 portions of cabecou (soft goat cheese)
- dried thyme
- pepper
- sea salt (fleur de sel)

Cabecou parcels with a leek fondue & button mushroom carpaccio

Economical

Preparation: 20 min – Cooking time: 15 min

Preheat the oven to 180°C (350°F) (th. 6). Finely slice, wash, and drain the leeks. Clean the mushrooms with a brush and cut them into thin, round slices. Squeeze the lemon juice over the mushrooms to prevent them from discoloring. Chop the parsley.

Heat the oil in a frying pan and sauté the leeks for 3 minutes, turning them frequently. Season with salt and cover. Leave to simmer over a low heat for 5 minutes. Remove the pan from the heat, add half of the parsley, and stir.

Spread out the pastry sheets and place ¼ of the leeks and 1 portion of cabecou on each sheet. Sprinkle with thyme and pepper. Fold each side of the sheet to form a parcel. Brush a baking tray with some oil. Place the parcels on the tray and brush the tops of the parcels with oil. Place the tray in the oven and bake for 6 to 8 minutes until golden brown.

Place each parcel in the center of a plate. Arrange the mushrooms in a ring around the parcel and sprinkle them with sea salt and parsley. Serve immediately.

Suggested wine pairing: a white Sancerre (Loire Valley).

Serves 4

- 4 sheets of phyllo pastry
- 80 g (2¾ oz) arugula
- 100 g (3½ oz) Carré Frais (soft cream cheese)
- salt
- freshly ground pepper
- 4 dessert spoons (2¾ Tbsp) olive oil

Arugula cigars

Chic

Preparation: 20 min – Cooking time: 10 min

Preheat the oven to 210°C (410°F) (th. 7). Cut the phyllo pastry sheets in two. Coarsely chop the arugula and place it in a mixing bowl. Break up the Carré Frais with a fork and add to the bowl with salt, pepper, and half of the olive oil. Mix the ingredients.

Evenly distribute the arugula and Carré Frais mixture onto each sheet of phyllo pastry. Fold the longest sides of the sheet and roll it up into a cigar. Brush the cigars with the rest of the olive oil. Place the cigars on a parchment paper–lined baking tray and bake for about 10 minutes, until they are crisp and golden. Serve immediately.

Suggested wine pairing: a Muscadet (a Loire Valley white).

Choosing a cake pan

Silicone • **advantages:** no greasing required; easy removal; easy to clean; available in different shapes and sizes. • **disadvantages:** its flexibility makes it difficult to handle, especially when it's full of uncooked batter; cooking times may vary, depending on the quality of the silicone.

Steel with non-stick coating • **advantages:** easy to handle; guarantee of nice, golden cakes; shatterproof; very little greasing required (or none at all); easy to clean. • **disadvantages:** easy to damage the coating with a knife when checking the cooking process or removing the cake from the pan.

Tin • **advantages:** excellent heat conduction that gives a lovely golden color to pastry or batter; reasonably priced; shatterproof. • **disadvantages:** needs to be greased or lined to make removal easier; can be pitted with rust; it is a good idea to grease the cake pan before putting it away.

Glass or ceramic • **advantages:** withstands intensive use; scratchproof; easy to clean. • **disadvantages:** needs to be very well greased; breakable; when ooking cakes, the heat conduction is less effective than with a silicone or metal cake pan.

Serves 6

- 90 g (3 oz) smoked duck breast
- 80 g (2¾ oz) butter
- 6 eggs
- 200 g (7 oz) pre-cooked polenta
- 50 g (1¾ oz) flour
- 1 sachet (11 g / ¼ oz) of baking powder
- 1 pinch saffron powder
- 10 cL (½ cup) whipping or heavy cream (35%)
- 50 g (1¾ oz) tomates confit (or bottled sun-dried tomatoes)
- 150 g (5 oz) cooked corn kernels, drained
- salt
- pepper

Savory corn & smoked duck breast cake

Prepare in advance

Preparation: 10 min – Cooking time: 40 min

Preheat the oven to 180°C (350°F) (th. 6). Cut the duck breast into cubes. Melt the butter in the microwave or a saucepan.

Break the eggs into a mixing bowl and using an electric mixer, whisk until they become foamy. Stir in the polenta, flour, baking powder, and saffron. Continue stirring while adding the melted butter, heavy cream, and tomato dip.

Season to taste with salt and pepper. Finally, add the duck breast cubes and corn. Pour the mixture into a cake pan and bake in the oven for 40 minutes. Check the cooking process by inserting the blade of a knife into the cake; if the blade comes out clean, the cake is cooked. Leave the cake to cool before removing it from the pan. Cut the cake into slices or large cubes and serve cold as an appetizer.

Suggested wine pairing: a Côtes de Duras rosé (South West France).

CVF recommendation: The saffron can be replaced with paprika or Espelette pepper (in this case, do not add pepper).

Serves 4

- 8 large slices of white sandwich bread
- 40 g (1½ oz) soft butter
- 1 level dessert spoon (2 tsp) tomato paste
- Espelette pepper
- 3 plum tomatoes
- salt
- 200 g (7 oz) sheep's milk cheese (Ossau-iraty)

Mini cheese & tomato croque-monsieur sandwiches

Informal

Preparation: 20 min – Cooking time: 10 min

Remove the crust from each slice of bread. Using a fork, combine the soft butter, the tomato paste, and a touch of Espelette pepper. Spread this mixture over the slices of bread.

Wash and dry the tomatoes. Cut them into thin, round slices. Place them on a dish and sprinkle with table salt to remove any excess water. Let them stand for 5 minutes. Meanwhile, remove the rind and thinly slice the cheese.

Using a paper towel, gently wipe the tomato slices and place them on the 4 slices of bread. Add the cheese and place the buttered side of the 4 remaining slices of bread on top of the cheese.

Cook the croque-monsieur sandwiches in a Panini grill or a non-stick frying pan over low heat. Turn regularly until they are golden brown and the cheese has melted. Cut each sandwich diagonally in half and serve immediately.

Suggested wine pairing: a white Irouléguy (Basque Country).

Serves 4

- 2 eggplants
- 4 dessert spoons (2¾ Tbsp) olive oil
- 8 sprigs of basil
- 100 g (3½ oz) sun-dried tomatoes in oil (from a jar)
- 200 g (7 oz) Carré Frais (soft cream cheese)
- pepper

Eggplant & basil rolls

Chic

Preparation: 30 min – Cooking time: 10 min

Heat a cast iron grill. Wash the eggplants and cut them lengthwise into thin slices (discard the first and last slices, which are only skin). Brush both sides with oil and bake for 2 minutes per side under the broiler (only do a few at a time).

Chop the basil. Drain the tomatoes and dice. Using a fork, combine the cheese, basil, tomatoes, and one spoonful of their oil in a mixing bowl. Season with pepper.

Spread this filling over the eggplant slices and roll, not too tightly. Skewer each roll with a wooden cocktail stick and place in the refrigerator until serving.

Suggested wine pairing: a Côtes de Provence rosé.

Zucchini rolls with goat cheese

Inventive
Preparation: 30 min
Cooking time: 2 min

For 20 rolls

- 1 bunch dill
- 200 g (7 oz) creamy goat cheese (Petit Billy, Chavroux, or Vrai)
- freshly ground pepper
- 3 long, medium-sized zucchinis
- 1 small jar of salmon roe

Rinse, dry, and chop the dill. Mix the dill with the cheese in a bowl and add pepper to taste. Wash and wipe the zucchinis. Using a vegetable peeler, cut them into long strips. Blanch the zucchini for 2 minutes in salted, boiling water before immersing them in ice-cold water.

Place a teaspoonful of goat cheese on one end of each zucchini strip and roll. Use wooden cocktail sticks to hold the rolls together.

Place the rolls alongside each other on a serving dish and add a little salmon roe to each one. Cover with plastic wrap and place in the refrigerator until ready to serve.

CVF recommendation: Add small pieces of dried fruits, figs, or hazelnuts to the cheese filling. Chervil can be used instead of dill.

Suggested wine pairing: a Pays d'Oc IGP rosé.

Soups

Alsatian griess soup

Regional

Preparation: 20 min
Cooking time: 20 min

Serves 6

- 1 large onion
- 1 carrot
- 1 small celery stalk
- 1 leek (white part only)
- 100 g (3½ oz) smoked diced bacon (lardons)
- 40 g (1½ oz) butter
- 140 g (5 oz) coarse durum wheat semolina
- 2 dessert spoons (1¼ Tbsp) chicken bouillon powder
- 15 cL (⅔ cup) table cream (18%) or light cream (10%)
- salt
- pepper

Peel the onion and the carrot. Remove the celery strings and clean the leek. Cut the vegetables and bacon into tiny cubes.

Melt the butter in a saucepan. Add the semolina and stir until golden. Add the vegetable and bacon cubes and continue stirring for another 5 minutes. Pour in 1½ L (4 cups) of boiling water and add the bouillon powder. Stir and bring to a boil

Partially cover the saucepan, adjust the heat, and leave to simmer for 40 minutes. Add the cream, salt, and pepper. Stir and serve piping hot.

Suggested wine pairing: an Alsace pinot gris.

Cream of Stilton & bacon soup

Informal

Preparation: 20 min
Cooking time: 20 min

Serves 6

- 4 large starchy potatoes (bintje variety)
- 60 cL (2½ cups) milk
- 50 cL (2 cups) table cream (18%) or light cream (10%)
- 300 g (10 oz) Stilton, crumbled
- 12 very thin bacon slices
- 8 sprigs of flat-leaf parsley
- pepper

Crumble the Stilton. Peel the potatoes, cut them into cubes, and cook for 15 minutes in boiling water. Drain and transfer to a saucepan. Add the milk, cream, and crumbled Stilton. Puree the ingredients with a hand-held blender (or pour into an electric blender). Bring to a boil for 1 minute, and then keep warm over very low heat.

Fry the bacon in a non-stick frying pan, then crumble with your fingers. Remove the leaves from the parsley and chop. Pour the soup into bowls, sprinkle with bacon, add a little parsley and pepper, and serve immediately.

CVF recommendation : Stilton is an English blue-veined cheese. It can be replaced by Fourme d'Ambert or a similar blue cheese.

Suggested wine pairing : a Condrieu (Rhône Valley white).

Exotic coconut milk

Coconut milk can be purchased in cans or small cartons and is found in the Asian food section of the supermarket. It is also called coconut cream and is obtained from coconut flesh and water. You need to shake the carton or the can prior to opening to even out the liquid.

Combined with curry paste or curry powder, coconut milk is an ideal ingredient for tasty vegetable, chicken, or prawn curries. Its mildly sweet taste adds an Asian flavor to many different soups, including prawn, leek, onion, carrot, zucchini, coral lentil, and squash. It can also be used in sweet dishes, such as pancakes, rice puddings, clafoutis, smoothies, and cocktails.

It is gluten free and rich in calcium, potassium, phosphorous magnesium, copper, sulfur, iron, and B, C, and E group vitamins. There is, however, one drawback: it also contains significant levels of saturated fatty acids and carbohydrates.

Serves 6

- 300 g (10 oz) raw, medium-sized prawns (or frozen)
- 2 onions
- 2 garlic cloves
- 20 g ($^3/_4$ oz) fresh ginger
- 1 lemongrass stalk
- 2 dessert spoons (1¼ Tbsp) oil
- 2 small chili peppers
- 30 cL (1¼ cup) coconut milk
- salt
- 2 dessert spoons (1¼ Tbsp) fish bouillon powder
- 2 carrots
- juice of 1 lemon
- 20 cL ($^3/_4$ cup) table cream (18%) or light cream (10%)
- 6 sprigs of cilantro

Thai cream of prawn soup

Exotic

Preparation: 30 min – Cooking time: 30 min

Shell the prawns (after defrosting if frozen) and place in the refrigerator. Keep the heads and shells for the bouillon. Peel and finely chop the onions and garlic cloves. Peel and grate the ginger. Chop the lemongrass.

Pour the oil into a casserole dish. Add the prawn shells and heads, the onion and garlic, and stir until golden. Add the ginger, lemongrass, peppers, and coconut milk. Season with salt and stir. Add 75 cL (3¼ cups) of water and the fish bouillon powder. Leave to simmer for 20 minutes.

Peel and grate the carrots (with the large slots of the grater). Filter the bouillon and pour into the casserole dish. Add the prawns, carrots, lemon juice, and table cream. Leave to simmer for 10 minutes.

Pour the soup into bowls, sprinkle with cilantro, and serve hot.

Suggested wine pairing: a white Alsace pinot.

Split pea soup

Classic

Preparation: 20 min – Soaking: 1 h – Cooking time: 50 min

Serves 6

- 500 g (1 lb) split peas
- 3 garlic cloves
- 1 bay leaf
- 1 sprig of savory
- 2 chicken bouillon cubes
- salt
- 200 g (7 oz) cured ham in one slice
- 4 dessert spoons (2¾ Tbsp) olive oil
- 2 slices of stale white sandwich bread
- pepper

Soak the split peas for 1 hour in cold water. Drain the peas and transfer to a stew pot. Add 2 L (8 cups) of cold water, 1 peeled garlic clove, the bay leaf, savory, and chicken bouillon cubes. Bring to a boil then leave to simmer for 45 minutes. At the end of the cooking process, season with salt (very little) and remove both the bay leaf and the savory.

Meanwhile, cut the ham into thin strips. Peel and chop 1 garlic clove and mix with the ham. Heat a little oil in a frying pan and slowly fry the both until the garlic is transparent. Remove from the pan and gently pat with a paper towel.

Mix the stew pot ingredients with a hand-held blender or an electric blender until the mixture is smooth and creamy. Transfer the mixture back into the stew pot and keep warm.

Cut the bread into small cubes. Rub each cube with the last peeled garlic clove and fry in the olive oil.

Before serving, add a little pepper and a drizzle of oil. Serve in soup bowls and sprinkle with the ham and fried bread cubes.

Suggested wine pairing: a red Beaujolais Villages.

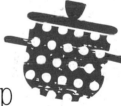

Cream of endive & smoked duck breast soup

Prepare in advance

Preparation: 15 min – Cooking time: 20 min

Serves 4

- 2 chicken bouillon cubes
- 6 endives
- 2 potatoes
- 90 g (3 oz) dried and sliced duck breast
- 10 cL (½ cup) heavy cream (35%)
- ½ dessert spoon (1 tsp) superfine (berry) sugar
- salt
- pepper
- chives

Dilute the bouillon cubes in 80 cL (3½ cups) of boiling water. Wash and cut the endives into round slices. Peel and cut the potatoes into cubes. Add the vegetables to the boiling water and leave to simmer for 20 minutes.

Meanwhile, trim the fat from the edges of the duck breast slices and set aside. Remove the soup from the heat. Add the cream and sugar and mix (either with an electric blender or a hand-held blender) until the soup is smooth and creamy. Season with salt and pepper.

Transfer the soup to serving bowls. Sprinkle with the finely chopped chives and, finally, add the slices of duck breast. Serve piping hot.

CVF recommendation: You can replace the duck breast with very thin slices of fried smoked bacon.

Suggested wine pairing: a white Bergerac (South West France).

Rediscover the virtues of lentils

Lentils are a highly recommended source of nutrition. Not only are they rich in iron, fiber, proteins, and minerals, they are also easily digestible. Legumes have the reputation of being tedious to cook, but this is not the case with lentils. They don't need to be soaked and cook quickly – in only 25 minutes. If overcooked, however, they become floury, disintegrate, and lose their delicate flavor.

Coral lentils are red decorticated lentils that are very popular in North African and Indian cuisine. They cook in less than 15 minutes and can be used for thickening soups, purées, and fillings. Green lentils are produced in several areas in France, notably in the regions of Berry and Auvergne.

A warm lentil salad with shallots, diced smoked bacon or lardons, parsley, and a poached egg is delicious. Lentils can also be used in soups or served with smoked sausage – Morteau sausage, for example, or salt pork (petit salé).

Serves 4

- 120 g (4¼ oz) coral lentils
- 1 portion pumpkin (400 g / 14 oz)
- 1 onion
- 1 dessert spoon (2 tsp) olive oil
- 1 pinch ground cumin
- ½ chicken bouillon cube
- 10 cL (½ cup) coconut milk
- salt
- pepper
- 4 pinches shredded coconut
- 2 sprigs cilantro

Cream of coral lentil & pumpkin soup

Vitality

Preparation: 10 min – Cooking time: 20 min

Rinse and drain the lentils. Peel and slice the pumpkin into cubes. Peel and chop the onion. Lightly brown the onion in a frying pan with a spoonful of oil and then sprinkle with cumin.

Add the pumpkin cubes and the lentils and stir with a spatula for 3 minutes. Dilute the chicken bouillon in 50 cL (2 cups) of hot water and pour into the frying pan. Bring to a boil. Reduce the heat, add the coconut milk, a little salt, and stir. Cover and cook for 15 to 20 minutes (the lentils should be tender).

Mix the ingredients in a blender with the remaining oil (add a little water, if necessary). Season with pepper and serve in four soup bowls. Sprinkle with shredded coconut, top with cilantro, and serve.

Suggested wine pairing: a white Côtes de Gascogne.

Cream of pumpkin soup

Informal

Preparation : 10 min
Cooking time : 40 min

Serves 4

- 1.5 kg (2 lb) pumpkin
- 1 garlic clove
- 1 clove
- 1 sprig of thyme
- 1 L (4 cups) milk
- 1 pinch nutmeg
- salt
- pepper
- 3 fresh or frozen sheets of ravioles de Royans (tiny ravioli filled with a blend of cheese and herbs)
- 4 dessert spoons (2¾ Tbsp) mascarpone
- 10 chive sprigs

Remove the skin and seeds from the pumpkin. Slice the pulp into cubes. Peel the garlic and wrap it in a piece of gauze with the thyme and the clove.

Pour the milk into a stew pot. Add the gauze with the seasoning, the pumpkin, nutmeg, salt, and pepper. Bring to a boil, cover, and leave to simmer over low heat for 30 minutes. Stir occasionally.

Remove the gauze and pour the ingredients into a blender. Mix until smooth and creamy. Transfer the soup back into the stew pot and add a little water if the soup is too thick. Bring to the boil and add the ravioli sheets. Cook for 1 minute.

Chop the chives. Spoon the soup and the ravioli into four soup bowls. Garnish with the chopped chives and a spoonful of mascarpone. Serve immediately.

CVF recommendation : Stilton is an English blue-veined cheese. It can be replaced by Fourme d'Ambert or a similar blue cheese.

Suggested wine pairing: a dry Montlouis (a Loire Valley white).

(Photo page 30)

Serves 4

- 1 shallot
- 500 g (1 lb) button mushrooms
- 1 dessert spoon (2 tsp) olive oil
- salt
- 150 g (5 oz) peeled chestnut (frozen or jarred)
- 1 vegetable bouillon cube
- 8 cL (⅓ cup) low-fat milk
- 1 heaped dessert spoon (2 tsp) hazelnut paste (try Jean Hervé)
- pepper
- 12 hazelnuts
- 4 vacherin (or fontina or emmenthal) cheese slivers

Cream of mushroom, chestnut, hazelnut & cheese soup

Vegetarian

Preparation: 10 min – Cooking time: 20 min

Peel and chop the shallot. Brush the mushrooms to remove the dirt and slice. Heat the oil in a heavy-bottomed stew pot over a medium heat. Add the chopped shallot and a pinch of salt and stir until the shallot becomes transparent. Add the mushrooms and stir continuously for about 5 minutes. Set aside some mushrooms for later.

Add water to cover the ingredients in the stew pot, then add the chestnuts and the vegetable bouillon cube. Cover and cook over low heat for 10 minutes. Remove the stew pot from the heat and add the milk, the hazelnut paste, and pepper. Mix and check the seasoning.

Dry roast the hazelnuts and grind into a coarse powder.

Pour the hot soup into four mugs (or soup bowls). Add a sliver of vacherin cheese, garnish with the reserved mushrooms, and sprinkle with ground hazelnuts.

Suggested wine pairing: a white Arbois (Jura).
(Photo page 31)

Serves 4

- 500 g (1 lb) button mushrooms
- 100 g (3½ oz) porcini mushrooms
- 2 shallots
- 20 g (¾ oz) walnut kernels
- 2 chicken bouillon cubes
- 20 g (¾ oz) low-fat butter (for cooking)
- salt
- pepper
- 15 cL (⅔ cup) light cream (10%) or table cream (18%)
- 1 dessert spoon (2 tsp) walnut oil

Creamy mushroom & walnut soup

Vitality

Preparation : 20 min – Cooking time : 15 min

Clean the mushrooms by rapidly brushing them under cold water. Gently pat dry before thinly slicing. Peel and chop the shallots. Crush the walnut kernels. Dilute the bouillon cubes in 1 L (4 cups) of boiling water.

Melt the butter in a frying pan and sauté the mushrooms. Season with salt and pepper. When all the water has evaporated, remove the mushrooms from the pan and cook the shallots.

Combine the mushrooms, shallots, cream, and hot bouillon in a blender until you obtain a frothy mixture. Transfer to soup bowls, drizzle with walnut oil, and sprinkle with the crushed walnut kernels. Serve hot.

Suggested wine pairing: a Savoie Chignin-Bergeron.

Salads

- 300 g (10 oz) green lentils
- 1 garlic clove
- 1 onion
- 1 carrot
- 1 bunch mixed herbs (thyme, bay leaf, parsley)
- 6 eggs
- 200 g (7 oz) diced smoked bacon (or lardons)
- 2 dessert spoons (1¼ Tbsp) balsamic vinegar
- 4 dessert spoons (2¾ Tbsp) olive oil
- salt
- pepper
- 2 pinches of curry powder

Curried lentil, bacon & egg salad

Vitality

Preparation : 30 min – Cooking time : 30 min

Place the lentils in a colander. Rinse, drain, and transfer them to a stew pot. Peel the garlic and the onion. Peel and chop the carrot into round slices. Add these ingredients and the bunch of herbs to the lentils. Cover with cold water and leave to simmer for 25 to 30 minutes.

Meanwhile, gently place the eggs in simmering water. Leave them to cook for 7 minutes if they are cold or 6 minutes if they are at room temperature. Once they are cooked, quickly cool under cold running water and peel off the shells.

In a non-stick frying pan, sauté the diced bacon for 3 minutes over high heat. Combine the vinegar, oil, salt, pepper, and curry in a bowl.

Remove the bunch of herbs, the garlic and onion from the stew pot. Drain the lentils and the carrot and transfer to a salad dish. Add the vinaigrette, toss, and divide among the plates. Place an egg on top, sprinkle with the diced bacon, and serve warm.

Suggested wine pairing: a red Côtes D'auvergne.

The top 10 spices for every kitchen

A few pinches of a well-chosen spice add character and color to any dish. Spices can complement a variety of food – here are some great flavor pairings:

Pink peppercorns: add at the end of the cooking process to white fish, chicken, veal, sautéed or grilled duck breast; fish or steak tartare; meat and fish marinades.

Cinnamon: apple, pear, dried fruit or chocolate desserts; rice pudding; crème brûlée; custard tart; tagines; beef or lamb stuffings; tomato and meat sauces.

Cumin: dishes with cooked tomatoes; braised pork, beef, or lamb; grilled meatballs, tagines; lentils; eggplants; carrots; cabbage; potatoes; goat cheese.

Turmeric: rice; bulgur, dried vegetables; fish; shellfish; tagines; Asian cooking.

Curry: rice; lentils; vinaigrette for avocado; pork, chicken, turkey, lamb, or veal (with or without coconut milk); monkfish and other white fish; leeks; carrots; red kuri squash; potatoes; zucchini.

Ginger: raw, marinated, or foil-baked fish; chicken, duck, and veal; leeks; cabbage; onions (braised, cooked in a wok or in soup); fruits (compote, finely chopped, baked, or in a salad); gingerbread.

Nutmeg: potatoes, eggs, or melted cheese.

Paprika: breaded veal, chicken, turkey cutlets, or fish fillets; mussels; sautéed prawns; crab; sautéed veal or beef; roast chicken; cooked or cold tomato dishes; ratatouille; potato salad; coddled eggs or omelet; meatballs; mayonnaise.

Espelette pepper: can be used to replace pepper in marinades and to season meat, seafood, and fish; stuffings; cooked tomatoes and peppers; puff or shortcrust pastry cheese rolls.

Saffron: rice; pasta; white fish sauces and scallops; fish soup; prawn bouillons with chicken; pear desserts; fruit salads.

Serves 4

- 1 chicken bouillon cube
- pepper
- 2 free-range chicken breasts
- 200 g (7 oz) Swiss cheese
- 1 bunch green grapes
- 1 celery stalk
- 1 Granny Smith apple
- juice of ½ a lemon
- 50 g (1¾ oz) walnut kernels

For the dressing:

- ½ dessert spoon (1 tsp) mustard
- 1 egg yolk
- salt
- pepper
- 15 cL (⅔ cup) peanut oil
- 1 dessert spoon (2 tsp) ketchup
- Tabasco sauce

Chef's Swiss cheese salad

Prepare in advance

Preparation: 25 min – Cooking time: 10 min

Dilute the bouillon cube in ½ L (2 cups) of boiling water. Add pepper and the chicken breasts, cover, and cook for 10 minutes. Drain the chicken (keep a little bouillon for later) and cool.

Cut the cheese into cubes. Wash the grapes and remove them from the stalks. Remove the top portion of the celery and cut the stalk two-thirds of the way down so that only the tender part is left. Cut this "heart" into short sticks. Wash the apple and grate using the medium-sized grating slots. Sprinkle with lemon juice to prevent from discoloring.

Sauté the walnuts in a frying pan and set aside on a paper towel.

Prepare the dressing. Beat the mustard, egg yolk, salt, and pepper in a bowl. Slowly add the oil and keep beating. Once the mayonnaise is thick, add the ketchup, Tabasco sauce, and 2 dessert spoons (1¼ Tbsp) of chicken bouillon.

Thinly slice the chicken. Place the chicken, cheese, walnuts, grapes, celery, and apple in a salad bowl. Add the dressing and gently toss. Serve cold.

Suggested wine pairing: a Bourgogne Irancy (a red Burgundy).

Serves 4

- 200 g (7 oz) bulgur
- 1 small can of sliced pineapple in its own juice
- 1 small celery stalk
- ½ a smoked chicken
- 100 g (3½ oz) lamb's lettuce
- juice of 1 lemon
- 4 dessert spoons (2¾ Tbsp) olive oil
- salt
- pepper

Warm bulgur & smoked chicken salad

Vitality

Preparation: 20 min – Cooking time: 12 min

Sauté the bulgur on medium in a dessert spoon (2 tsp) of olive oil. Add twice its volume in water. Stir from time to time. From the moment the water starts boiling, it takes 10 to 12 minutes for it to evaporate completely and for the bulgur to be cooked. Once the bulgur is cooked, separate the grains with a fork.

Drain the pineapple and cut into short "sticks." Remove the celery strings and cut the celery into tiny cubes. Remove the skin and bones from the chicken and shred the meat. Prepare the lamb's lettuce.

Transfer the bulgur to a salad bowl. Add the lemon juice and olive oil and season with salt and pepper. Add the celery, pineapple, lamb's lettuce, and chicken. Gently toss and serve.

Suggested wine pairing: a Vouvray (Loire Valley).

Fennel & goat cheese salad

Light
Preparation : 20 min

Serves 4

- 2 fennel bulbs
- 1 small bunch red or black grapes
- 75 g (2⅔ oz) shelled, salted hazelnuts
- ½ a goat cheese log
- 2 dessert spoons (1¼ Tbsp) hazelnut oil
- 2 dessert spoons (1¼ Tbsp) neutral cooking oil (such as vegetable)
- 1 dessert spoon (2 tsp) sherry vinegar
- ½ dessert spoon (1 tsp) liquid honey
- salt • pepper

Wash and remove the outer layers of the fennel bulbs. Cut the bulbs into very thin slices, preferably using a mandolin. (Keep some of the green to garnish). Place the slices in a deep dish.

Rinse and dry the grapes. Coarsely crush the hazelnuts and cut the goat cheese into slivers.

Using a fork, combine the two oils, vinegar, honey, salt, and pepper in a mixing bowl. Pour the vinaigrette over the fennel and gently toss.

Before serving, add the goat cheese, hazelnuts, and grapes and gently toss. Garnish with the fennel greens and serve.

Suggested wine pairing: a Muscadet (a Loire Valley white).

Potato salad

Informal

Preparation: 40 min – Cooking time: 25 min

Serves 6

- 600 g (1¼ lb) large potatoes (Charlotte variety)
- 1 dessert spoon (2 tsp) coarse sea salt
- 350 g (⅔ lb) thickly sliced boiled ham
- 12 cherry tomatoes
- 2 sprigs of chervil
- 6 gherkins
- 1 very fresh egg yolk
- 1 dessert spoon (2 tsp) mustard
- salt • pepper
- 30 cL (1¼ cup) grapeseed oil
- ½ dessert spoon (1 tsp) wine vinegar

Wash the potatoes and place them in a large saucepan with 1 dessert spoon (2 tsp) of coarse sea salt. Cover with cold water and bring to a boil. Reduce the heat and leave to simmer for about 25 minutes (they should be soft in the center). Drain, cool, peel, and cut into round slices ½ cm (¼ inch) thick.

Slice the boiled ham into large, 2-cm (¾ inch) cubes. Wash and halve the cherry tomatoes. Remove the leaves from the chervil. Halve the gherkins lengthwise.

Prepare the dressing. Combine the egg yolk and the mustard in a mixing bowl. Season with salt and pepper. Using a hand or electric whisk, slowly add the oil. When the dressing is smooth and creamy, add the vinegar.

Transfer the potatoes to a salad bowl. Carefully stir in the dressing. Add the diced ham, gherkins, and cherry tomatoes. Garnish with the chervil sprigs. Serve immediately.

Suggested wine pairing: an Alsace pinot noir.

- 4 very fresh eggs
  (at room temperature)
- 1 shallot
- salt
- freshly ground pepper
- 1 dessert spoon (2 tsp) sherry
  vinegar
- 3 dessert spoons (2 Tbsp) olive oil
- 150 g (5 oz) lamb's lettuce
- 1 small bunch chives
- 15 cL (⅔ cup) peanut oil
- 240 g (½ lb) frozen, loose
  (not sheets) ravioles de Royans
  (tiny ravioli filled with a blend of
  cheese and herbs)

Crispy ravioli salad

Quick

Preparation : 20 min – Cooking time : 7 min

Boil some salted water in a saucepan, carefully add the eggs and leave to simmer for 5 minutes. Drain the eggs and cool in cold water. Carefully remove the shells without damaging the eggs.

Chop the shallot. Mix the shallot, salt, pepper, vinegar, and olive oil in a salad bowl. Add the lamb's lettuce, toss, and transfer to serving plates or bowls. Sprinkle with chopped chives.

Heat the peanut oil in a large saucepan. Add the frozen ravioli and cook until golden, about 2 minutes.

Drain the ravioli and add to the salad. Just before serving, make a slit in the eggs and add to the salad.

Suggested wine pairing: a Jacquère Savoy.

Great ideas for cheese

A cheese platter is always a tempting choice, but cheeses can also be used in a variety of ways. Some wonderful combinations are:

Fromage frais (fresh curd cheese) made from goat's milk or cow's milk: with phyllo pastry or puff pastry rolls; meat stuffings; savory tarts or savory cakes.

Parmesan: try shavings with arugula, lamb's lettuce, or young spinach leaves; grated and mixed with breadcrumbs for breaded fish; in basil, arugula, or lamb's lettuce pesto, or in the pastry of a tomato crumble.

Comté: try it cubed and sprinkled with paprika as an appetizer; in mushroom and bacon muffins; or in crème brûlée with cumin.

Mimolette: in endive salads or burgers.

Cantal: in cabbage parcels; croque-monsieur sandwiches; or with chicken breasts.

Roquefort: in pasta and meat sauces; endive or lamb's lettuce salads; or with coddled eggs.

Serves 6

- 150 g (5 oz) spicy chorizo
- 24 cherry tomatoes (preferably coeur de pigeon)
- 1 bunch chives
- freshly ground pepper
- 24 mozzarella balls (preferably buffalo)

Colorful mini-brochettes

Light

Preparation: 20 min – Cooking time: 10 min

Peel off the skin from the chorizo and cut the sausage into ½-cm (¼ inch) thick slices. Sauté in a frying pan, turning regularly. Drain with a skimmer. Cool on a paper towel.

Meanwhile, wash and dry the cherry tomatoes. Rinse, pat dry, and chop the chives. Place the chives in a deep dish, add pepper, and mix.

Drain the mozzarella balls and roll them in the chive/pepper mixture.

Thread the ingredients alternately onto 24 skewers: 1 slice of chorizo, 1 mozzarella ball, 1 cherry tomato, and 1 slice of chorizo. Serve the mini-brochettes at room temperature.

Suggested wine pairing: a white Patrimonio (Corsica).

(Photo page 44)

- 150 g (5 oz) peeled fava beans (frozen)
- 450 g (16 oz) mixed grilled vegetables (defrost if frozen)
- 60 g (2 oz) salted peanuts
- salt
- pepper
- 2 dessert spoons (1¼ Tbsp) balsamic vinegar
- 4 dessert spoons (2¾ Tbsp) olive oil
- 50 g (1¾ oz) arugula

Grilled vegetable & peanut salad

Prepare in advance

Preparation: 15 min – Cooking time: 10 min

Immerse the beans for 7 to 8 minutes in a saucepan of salted, boiling water. Drain and rinse in cold water (so they keep their color). Slice all the grilled vegetables into thin slivers and pat dry with a paper towel.

In a non-stick frying pan, lightly brown the peanuts. Leave them to cool on a paper towel and then coarsely crush.

In a salad bowl, combine the salt, pepper, vinegar, and oil with a fork. Add the vegetable slices, beans, and arugula. Gently toss, sprinkle with the crushed peanuts, and serve.

Suggested wine pairing: a Costières de Nîmes rosé (Rhône valley).

(Photo page 45)

Tarts

Onion & goat cheese tart

Economical

Preparation : 20 min
Cooking time : 35 min

Serves 6

- 3 bunches of scallions
- 3 dessert spoons (2 Tbsp) olive oil
- 1 dessert spoon (2 tsp) superfine (berry) sugar
- salt • freshly ground pepper
- 3 sprigs of rosemary • 1 sheet of puff pastry
- 200 g (7 oz) fromage frais (fresh curd cheese) (Petit Billy or Chavroux)
- 1 bunch chives

Peel the scallions and cut into chunks, keeping some of the stalk. Heat 2 dessert spoons (1¼ Tbsp) of oil in a frying pan, and, stirring frequently, brown the scallions. Sprinkle with sugar. Add salt, pepper, 10 to 15 cL (½ to ⅔ cup) of water, and the rosemary leaves. Leave to simmer, uncovered, for 15 minutes or until the onions are soft and caramelized.

Meanwhile, preheat the oven to 210°C (410°F) (th. 7). Roll out the dough with its parchment paper and place on a baking tray. Prick the dough with a fork and brush with the rest of the olive oil. Put in the oven and blind bake for about 20 minutes, until the pastry is golden brown.

Rinse, dry, and chop the chives. In a bowl, break up the cheese with a fork. Place the tart on a serving dish and add the cheese, then the onions. Sprinkle with the chopped chives and serve immediately.

Suggested wine pairing: a Vin de Pays d'Oc muscat.

Maxi zucchini pizza

Informal

Preparation: 30 min – Cooking time: 15 min

Serves 6

For the pesto:
• 1 bunch basil • 50 g (1¾ oz) Parmesan, diced
• 50 g (1¾ oz) pine nuts • juice of 1 lemon • salt • pepper
• 10 cL (½ cup) olive oil

For the pizza:
• 1 thick rectangular sheet of pizza dough
• 3 small zucchinis • 3 dessert spoons (2 Tbsp) olive oil
• salt • pepper • 1 mozzarella ball
• 3 white onions with stalks • 12 cherry tomatoes
• 6 thin slices cured ham • 1 bunch chives

Prepare the pesto. Place the basil leaves, Parmesan, pine nuts, lemon juice, salt, and pepper in the food processor. Mix, stop, add a little oil, and mix again. Repeat these steps until the mixture is smooth and creamy.

Preheat the oven to 210 °C (410°F) (th. 7). Cover a baking tray with parchment paper and spread the dough over the paper. Wash and dry the zucchinis. Discard each end and slice into tiny cubes. Sauté for 3 minutes in a frying pan with 1 dessert spoon (2 tsp) of oil over high heat, stirring regularly. Add salt and pepper.

Cut the mozzarella into round slices. Peel and coarsely chop the onions with their stalks. Wash, dry, and quarter the tomatoes.

Spread the pesto over the dough. Add, in the following order, the ham, mozzarella, diced zucchinis, onions, and tomatoes. Season with salt and pepper, add a dash of oil, and bake in the oven for 10 to 12 minutes. Remove the pizza from the oven and sprinkle with the chopped chives. Cut the pizza and serve immediately.

Suggested wine pairing: a Côtes de Duras rosé (South West France).

Serves 4

- 1 sheet puff pastry
- 20 g (¾ oz) butter
- 3 dessert spoons (2 Tbsp) chopped shallots (fresh or frozen)
- 500 g (1 lb) skinned, salmon olive oil
- 1 bunch cilantro
- salt
- pepper
- 2 dessert spoons (1¼ Tbsp) olive oil
- 1 egg yolk, beaten

Salmon & cilantro pies

Original

Preparation: 15 min
Cooking time: 25 min

Leave the pastry in the refrigerator so that it is very cold (it will rise much better during the baking process). Preheat the oven to 210°C (410°F) (th. 7). Melt the butter in a frying pan and, over a low heat, sauté the shallots for 5 minutes.

Cut the salmon into large cubes and remove the leaves from the cilantro stems. Transfer the shallots to a mixing bowl. Add the salmon and the cilantro leaves. Stir in salt, pepper, and a dash of olive oil.

Divide the mixture equally into four, ovenproof ramekins. Roll out the cold dough and cut out four circles that are a little larger than the diameter of the ramekin.

Place these dough "lids" on the ramekins and firmly squeeze the edges so that they stick firmly. Brush the dough with the beaten egg yolk and bake for 15 to 20 minutes, or until the pastry rises and turns golden brown. Serve immediately.

Suggested wine pairing: a white Graves (Bordeaux).

Serves 6

- 20 pink radishes
- 400 g (14 oz) shelled peas
- 10 sprigs of chervil or dill
- 2 handfuls baby spinach
- 15 g (½ oz) butter + 10 g (⅓ oz) for the pie dish
- 4 eggs
- 50 cL (2 cups) table cream (18%) or light cream (10%)
- salt
- freshly ground pepper
- 20 g (¾ oz) flour (for the counter)
- 300 g (10 oz) shortcrust (pie crust) pastry (see recipe on following page) or 1 ready-to-use crust
- 200 g (7 oz) diced smoked bacon (or lardons)

Spring vegetable tart

Prepare in advance

Preparation: 20 min – Cooking time: 50 min

Preheat the oven to 180°C (350°F) (th. 6) and grease the pie dish. Clean and cut the radishes into round slices. Cook the peas for 5 minutes in boiling, salted water. Add the radishes and cook for another 2 minutes. Drain the vegetables and place them under cold running water (so they keep their color).

Rinse, pat dry, remove the leaves, and finely chop the chervil or dill. Rinse and pat dry the spinach. Put the spinach in a frying pan with the butter and cook for 2 minutes until it reduces. In a salad bowl, whisk the eggs and cream. Add the chopped herb and the vegetables. Season with salt and pepper.

Flour the counter. Roll out the dough, prick with a fork, and place in a pie dish with the pricked side facing down. Pour the ingredients over the dough and sprinkle with the diced bacon (or lardons). Bake for about 45 minutes. Serve warm or hot.

Suggested wine pairing: a white Alsace pinot.

Shortcrust pastry recipe

For 300 g (10 oz) of pastry:

Place 200 g (7 oz) of flour, 100 g (3½ oz) of cold, cubed butter, and a pinch of salt in a salad bowl. Rub the butter with your fingertips and crumble with the flour. Slowly add a trickle of water while kneading the dough into a flat ball. To obtain the best texture, avoid kneading for too long. Wrap the dough in plastic wrap and place in the refrigerator for at least 30 minutes. Remove the dough from the refrigerator shortly before rolling it out onto a floured counter.

Flavored shortcrust pastry

Reinvent a classic tart by adding an extra flavor, some color, and an original twist to the dough.

Tomato pastry: at the end of the dough-making process, add 50 g (1¾ oz) of well-drained, mixed, tomatoes confit (or bottle of sun-dried tomatoes).

Herb pastry: at the end of the dough-making process, add a finely chopped herb: parsley, basil, or tarragon.

Tapenade pastry (olive paste): replace 40 g (1½ oz) of butter with green olive tapenade and leave out the salt.

Balsamic vinegar pastry: replace half of the water with balsamic vinegar and leave out the salt.

Spinach & goat cheese calzone

Economical

Preparation : 25 min
Cooking time : 10 min

Serves 4

- 250 g (½ lb) mozzarella
- 1 kg (2 lb) defrosted spinach
- 200 g (7 oz) fresh goat cheese (Soignon or Petit Billy)
- salt • pepper
- pinch nutmeg
- 2 round sheets of pizza dough

Preheat the oven to 210°C (410°F) (th. 7). Dice the mozzarella. Wring out the excess water from the spinach and chop with a knife. Wring out the spinach again and transfer to a salad bowl.

Break up the goat cheese with a fork and add to the salad bowl with the diced mozzarella. Season with salt, pepper, and nutmeg.

Roll out the pizza dough on parchment paper and place on a baking tray. Spread the mixture on half of the round portions of dough. Wrap with the other half of the dough to form a folded pizza (calzone). Pinch the edges with wet fingers.

Bake in the oven for 10 minutes, or until the dough is golden brown. Cut each calzone in half and serve immediately.

Suggested wine pairing: a white Saint Véran (Burgundy).

- 1 sheet of 100% pure butter puff pastry
- 1 small bunch flat-leaf parsley
- 1 shallot
- 500 g (1 lb) button mushrooms
- 20 g (¾ oz) butter
- salt
- pepper
- 6 thin slices smoked duck breast
- 3 eggs
- 20 cL (¾ cup) heavy cream (35%)

Mushroom & smoked duck breast quiche

Prepare in advance
Preparation: 20 min
Cooking time: 50 min

Preheat the oven to 210°C (410°F) (th. 7). Roll out the pastry and its parchment paper to fit a round or rectangular pie dish. Prick the dough with a fork and blind bake for 10 to 12 minutes.

Wash, dry, and remove the leaves from the parsley. Peel and chop the shallot and the parsley and mix together. Brush the mushrooms under slow, running water to remove the dirt. Pat dry and thinly slice.

Melt the butter in a frying pan and when the pan is very hot, add the sliced mushrooms. Cook and stir for 5 minutes until the water has completely evaporated. Add salt and pepper.

Cut the smoked duck breast into thin slices. In a salad bowl, beat the eggs and fold in the cream. Add the duck breast, the sautéed mushrooms, and salt and pepper to taste. Pour the mixture over the pre-baked tart. Reduce the oven temperature to 180°C (350°C) (th. 6) and bake for 35 minutes.

Remove the pan from the heat and stir in the parsley and shallot mixture.

Serve hot with, for example, an arugula salad seasoned with chervil, tarragon, chives, or cilantro.

Suggested wine pairing: a red Santenay (Burgundy).

Serves 6

- 500 g (1 lb) apples
- 60 g (2 oz) butter
- salt
- pepper
- pinch allspice
- 12 very thin slices of smoked streaky bacon
- 2 eggs
- 15 cL (⅔ cup) heavy cream (35%)
- 15 cL (⅔ cup) milk
- 20 g (¾ oz) flour (for the counter)
- 300 g (10 oz) or 1 sheet of shortcrust (pie crust) pastry
- 8 pitted prunes
- 30 g (1 oz) superfine (berry) sugar

Bacon, apple & prune quiche

Inventive

Preparation: 30 min
Cooking time: 50 min

Peel the apples, remove the cores and seeds, and dice. Melt 50 g (1¾ oz) of butter in a frying pan. Add the apples and sugar and cook slowly until all the liquid has evaporated. Add salt, pepper, and allspice to the compote and set aside.

Sauté the bacon slices in a non-stick frying pan over a high heat for 2 minutes. Thinly slice the prunes.

Preheat the oven to 180°C (350°F) (th. 6) and grease a pie dish. Roll out the dough on a floured counter (if you are using a sheet of dough, roll out with the parchment paper) and place in the pie dish. Prick the dough with a fork.

In a mixing bowl, beat the eggs, cream, and milk. Add salt (but very little because of the bacon) and pepper. Spread the bacon slices across the bottom of the quiche.

Cover with the apple compote and the prune slices. Top with the egg and cream mixture. Bake for about 35 minutes or until the pastry is golden brown. Serve hot with a batavia lettuce and shallots.

Suggested pairing: a dry farm cider.

Gratins

Leek & ham gratin

Economical

Preparation: 25 min
Cooking time: 45 min

Serves 6

- 6 large leeks (or 12 medium sized)
- 1 chicken bouillon cube
- 50 g (1¾ oz) Comté cheese
- 40 g (1½ oz) butter + 10 g (⅓ oz) for the dish
- 1 dessert spoon (2 tsp) flour
- 40 cL (1¾ cups) milk
- grated nutmeg
- salt • pepper
- 6 slices boiled ham

Peel the leeks and discard two-thirds of the green part. Slit each leek into four but keep it whole. Rinse in water several times. In a stew pot, dilute the bouillon cube in boiling water. Add the leeks and leave to simmer for 15 to 20 minutes. Use a knife to check if the heart (the white part) is cooked; it should be tender. Allow the cooked leeks to drain thoroughly.

Preheat the oven to 180°C (350°F) (th. 6) and grease a gratin dish. Grate the cheese. Melt the butter in a thick-bottomed saucepan over low heat. As soon as the butter bubbles, slowly add the flour, stir for 1 minute, then gradually add the milk. Stir continuously until the white sauce thickens. Add the nutmeg and season with salt and pepper. Remove the pan from the heat and add half of the grated cheese.

Wrap 1 leek (or 2, depending on the size) in a slice of ham. Spread a little white sauce over the bottom of the dish. Place the leeks side by side and coat them with the rest of the sauce. Sprinkle with the remaining cheese. Bake in the oven for 25 minutes and serve.

Suggested wine pairing: a white Coteaux du Lyonnais.

- 250 g (8¾ oz) fresh porcini mushrooms
- 50 cL (2 cups) heavy cream (35%)
- 4 garlic cloves
- 1 sprig of thyme
- 1 bay leaf
- 1 whole nutmeg, for grating
- salt
- pepper
- 100 g (3½ oz) butter
- 400 g (14 oz) firm potatoes (Charlotte or Belle de Fontenay variety)

Potato & mushroom gratin

Chic

Preparation: 40 min – Cooking time: 1 h

Preheat the oven to 160°C (325°F) (th. 5-6). Brush and wash the mushroom stalks to remove the dirt and then carefully wipe dry. Remove the caps from the stalks and cut both parts into 5-mm (⅕ inch) thick slices, making sure that you keep the sliced caps and stalks separate from each other.

Pour the cream into a saucepan. Add the garlic cloves, thyme, bay leaf, a little grated nutmeg, salt, and pepper and bring to the boil. Simmer for 5 minutes. Using a small conical strainer, sieve the mixture to recover the cream.

Melt a knob of butter in a frying pan. Once the butter has turned golden brown, add the sliced mushroom caps, making sure they are evenly laid out in the pan, and sauté for 2 minutes over quite high heat. Remove the caps and repeat with the stalks. Cooking the caps and stalks separately is recommended because if there are too many mushrooms in the pan, they will not brown evenly.

Peel and rinse the potatoes. Cut them into 2-mm (1/16 inch) thick round slices.

Pour a thin layer of cream into a gratin dish. Then alternate as follows: a layer of potatoes, a layer of cream, a layer of mushrooms, and so on, finishing with a layer of potatoes.

Bake for 1 hour. Remove the gratin from the oven and serve immediately.

Suggested wine pairing: a Pauillac (a Bordeaux red).

Choosing the right potatoes

For gratins, stews, and oven-baked dishes:

• choose firm varieties, such as Amandine, Annabelle, Charlotte, Cherie, Franceline, Nicola, Pompadour, or Ratte, or baking potatoes, such as Agata, Monalisa, or Samba.

• Opt for baking potatoes to cook whole potatoes in the oven.

For French fries, mashed potatoes, and soups:

• choose starchy varieties, such as Artemis, Bintje, Caesar, Marabel, Melody, or Victoria.

Serves 6

- 500 g (1 lb) macaroni
- 60 cL (2½ cups) milk
- 20 g (¾ oz) butter
- 30 cL (1¼ cups) table cream (18%) or light cream (10%)
- salt
- pepper
- pinch nutmeg
- 200 g (7 oz) Swiss cheese (Emmental) or grated Parmesan

Traditional macaroni gratin

Economical

Preparation: 10 min
Resting time: 10 min
Cooking time: 30 min

Preheat the oven to 210°C (410°F) (th. 7). Boil a large quantity of salted water. Add the macaroni and cook for 8 minutes until it is al dente.

Meanwhile, boil the milk. Drain the pasta and transfer to a salad bowl. Pour the boiled milk over the macaroni and cover for 10 minutes so the pasta expands.

Transfer the macaroni to a greased gratin dish. Pour the cream over the pasta. Gradually add the salt, pepper, nutmeg, and half of the cheese. Top with the rest of the cheese and bake in the oven for 20 minutes or until the cheese is golden brown. Serve piping hot.

Suggested wine pairing: a white Côtes du Jura.

Florentine prawn gratin

Chic

Preparation: 30 min – Cooking time: 35 min

Serves 6

- 1 kg (2 lb) frozen spinach • 6 eggs • 50 g (1¾ oz) butter
- 30 g (1 oz) flour • 40 cL (1¾ cups) milk • salt • pepper
- pinch nutmeg • 20 cL (¾ cup) heavy cream (35%)
- 24 cooked, large prawns
- 80 g (2¾ oz) grated Parmesan

Defrost the spinach in a saucepan over low heat or in the microwave. At the same time, cook the eggs in a saucepan of boiling water with a pinch of salt (which will make them easier to shell) for 10 minutes until they are hard. Drain the eggs and allow them to cool. Shell the prawns.

Preheat the oven to 180°C (350°F) (th. 6) and grease an ovenproof dish.

Prepare the white sauce. Melt the remaining butter in a saucepan. Add the flour and stir firmly with a spatula until the mixture forms a ball. Cook for 1 minute while continuously turning it around with the spatula. Slowly add the milk and beat with a whisk until the sauce is smooth and creamy. Add the salt, pepper, and nutmeg and set aside.

Drain the spinach thoroughly and coarsely chop with a knife. Mix the spinach with the cream, season with salt and pepper, and transfer to the greased, ovenproof dish. Remove the shells from the eggs and cut them into thick, round slices. Spread them over the spinach, add the prawns, and coat with the white sauce. Sprinkle with Parmesan and bake in the oven for 20 minutes. Serve piping hot.

Suggested wine pairing: a white Côtes de Blaye (Bordeaux).

(Photo page 72)

Endive & creamy maroilles gratin

Regional

Preparation: 25 min – Cooking time: 1 h

Serves 4

- 1 kg (2 lb) endives
- 40 g (1½ oz) butter + 10 g (⅓ oz) for the dish
- 1 dessert spoon (2 tsp) superfine (berry) sugar • salt
- pepper • 20 g (¾ oz) flour • 30 cL (1¼ cups) milk
- 200 g (7 oz) Maroilles cheese

Remove the outer leaves of the endives, if necessary. Cut a cone out of the bottom of each endive to remove the hard core and cut in half lengthwise.

In a frying pan, melt 20 g (¾ oz) of butter and the sugar. Once the mixture starts bubbling, add the endives, salt, and pepper. Make sure to evenly coat the endives by turning them regularly. Cover and leave to simmer for 20 minutes. When cooked, remove the lid to allow the water to evaporate.

Meanwhile, melt the rest of the butter in a saucepan. Add the flour, and stir with a whisk while slowly adding the milk until it thickens. Season with salt and pepper.

Preheat the oven to 180°C (350ºF) (th. 6). Grease an ovenproof dish. Transfer the endives to the dish and coat with the sauce. Cut the cheese into thin slivers and lay over the sauce. Bake for 30 minutes, or until the cheese is golden brown. Serve piping hot.

Suggested pairing: an Abbey beer.

(Photo page 73)

Fish
&seafood

Mussels

Mussels are mainly farm cultured. They are bred on wooden pilings, known in French as bouchots, along the French Atlantic coast – from the Cotentin Peninsula to Charente.

Brittany, Normandy, the North Sea, the Loire, and Poitou-Charentes regions supply most of the French production. The bouchot mussels from the bay of Saint Michael's Mount have been granted Protected Designation of Origin (PDO).

Mussels are also bred in the Mediterranean. Spanish, Dutch, Irish, and Portuguese mussels are also popular. If they are bought live then they must be closed, or if they are half-open, they should close up when pressed. Mussels must be brushed and their byssal threads removed. They need to be washed several times, but not soaked in water. An average serving size per person is between 700 and 800 g (1½ lb) of mussels.

Serves 4

- 1 large onion
- 2 shallots
- 15 cL (⅔ cup) dry white wine
- 150 g (5 oz) smoked, diced bacon (or lardons)
- 15 cL (⅔ cup) heavy cream (35%)
- 10 cL (½ cup) light cream (10%)
- ½ bunch parsley
- 600 g (1¼ lb) sorted and cleaned mussels
- salt
- pepper

Mussels in a pot

Convivial

Preparation: 10 min – Cooking time: 20 min

Separately, peel, and finely chop the onion and shallots. Pour the white wine into a small saucepan, add the shallots and cook over low heat until only a little liquid remains.

Meanwhile, sauté the diced bacon for 5 minutes in a stew pot. Add the onions and cook for 5 minutes in the bacon fat. Add both creams and the shallots. Bring to a boil while stirring then lower the heat.

Wash, dry, and chop the parsley. Transfer the mussels to the pot. Add salt and pepper and heat for 5 minutes stirring continuously. Sprinkle with the chopped parsley and serve piping hot.

Suggested wine pairing: a white Patrimonio (Corsica).

Serves 4

- 2 kg (4½ lb) mussels
- 1 vegetable (or chicken) bouillon cube
- 30 cL (1¼ cups) coconut milk
- 1 onion
- 1 bunch cilantro
- 10 g (⅓ oz) butter
- salt
- pepper
- 1 dessert spoon (2 tsp) curry powder

Mussels in coconut milk

Inventive

Preparation: 20 min
Cooking time: 20 min

If necessary, meticulously brush the mussels under running water (although nowadays, mussels have usually already been cleaned). In a stew pot, dilute the bouillon cube in 50 cL (2 cups) of boiling water and add the coconut milk.

When the water boils, add the mussels and cook for about 10 minutes, stirring regularly until all the mussels have opened. While the mussels are cooking, peel and chop the onion. Remove the leaves from the cilantro and finely chop.

Drain the mussels by straining the bouillon, and keep the mussels warm. In a saucepan, melt the butter, add the onions, and cook until they are soft but not brown. Add the bouillon, a little salt, pepper, and curry powder. Simmer for about 10 minutes, or until the liquid thickens up.

Divide the mussels into four large bowls. Pour the coconut sauce over the top, sprinkle with the chopped cilantro, and serve immediately. White rice is an ideal side dish.

Suggested wine pairing: a dry Vouvray (a Loire Valley white).

Monkfish
& lime stew

Chic

Preparation : 20 min
Cooking time : 25 min

Serves 4

• 1 carrot • 300 g (10 oz) button mushrooms • 20 pearl onions
• 600 g (1¼ lb) monkfish (thick, round slices) • salt
• 2 dessert spoons (1¼ Tbsp) flour • 2 dessert spoons (1¼ Tbsp) olive oil
• 5 cL (¼ cup) Noilly-Prat (or dry white wine)

• 1 Ariake sachet seafood bouillon (or 1 dessert spoon / 2 tsp fish bouillon)
• pepper • 1 dessert spoon (2 tsp) cornstarch (Maïzena or Arrowroot powder)
• 8 cL (⅓ cup) low-fat milk • ½ dessert spoon (1 tsp) lime juice
• 3 dessert spoons (2 Tbsp) finely chopped flat-leaf parsley

Peel, wash, and cut the carrot into round slices. Brush the mushrooms under cool, running water and thinly slice. Peel the onions. Place the monkfish in a deep dish. Salt the fish, coat with flour, and tap lightly to remove any excess flour.

Heat the oil in a saucepan over medium heat. Add the fish and brown evenly on both sides. Add the onions, sliced carrot, and mushrooms. Pour in the Noilly-Prat, stir, and bring briefly to a boil. Add 10 cL (½ cup) of water, the bouillon, salt, and pepper and cover. Reduce the heat and simmer for 10 minutes.

In a bowl, combine the cornstarch and cold milk and, while stirring, add this mixture to the saucepan. Turn over the monkfish and add the lime juice. Keep stirring over a low heat until the sauce thickens up. Remove from the heat and sprinkle with the chopped parsley. Serve with brown rice.

Suggested wine pairing: a dry Vouvray (a Loire Valley white).

Whiting fillets baked in sea salt

Quick
Preparation: 20 min
Cooking time: 7 min

Serves 4

- 4 whiting fillets (200 g / 7 oz each) with skin on
- 1 kg (2¼ lb) sea salt • 1 sprig of thyme (preferably fresh)
- 2 dessert spoons (1¼ Tbsp) olive oil

Preheat the oven to 180°C (350°F) (th. 6). Pour the sea salt into an ovenproof dish and spread out in even layer.

Place the whiting fillets in the dish with the skin face down on the salt. Drizzle with a little olive oil and sprinkle with the thyme leaves. Bake in the oven for 7 minutes.

Remove the pink fillets, with a spatula and carefully peel off the skin with a sharp knife, making sure not to leave any sea salt on the fish. Serve immediately. Sautéed sugar snap peas are an ideal side dish.

Suggested wine pairing: a white Sancerre (Loire Valley).

- 1 celeriac bulb
- 2 potatoes (bintje variety)
- 2 shallots
- 2 onions
- 50 g (1¾ oz) butter
- 150 g (5 oz) chorizo
- 10 cL (½ cup) table cream (18%)
- 10 cL (½ cup) milk
- salt
- pepper
- 1 bunch chervil
- 900 g (2 lb) skinned and boned salmon fillets
- 3 dessert spoons (2 Tbsp) breadcrumbs

Salmon, celery & chorizo potato pie

Convivial

Preparation : 30 min – Cooking time : 1 h

Peel the celeriac and the potatoes. Cut them into cubes and cook in boiling, salted water for 25 minutes.

Meanwhile, peel and chop the shallots and onions. Cook over low heat with a knob of butter until they soften and become transparent (about 15 minutes). Cut the chorizo into thin, round slices, sauté briefly in a frying pan, and place on a paper towel to absorb some of the grease.

Drain the celeriac and potato cubes and blend. Stir in the cream, milk, salt, and pepper and set the purée aside. Remove the leaves from the chervil and finely chop.

Preheat the oven to 180°C (350ºF) (th. 6) and grease an ovenproof dish. Cut the salmon into slivers and place in the dish. Cover with the cooked onions, shallots, chorizo slices, half of the chervil, and finally, the purée. Sprinkle with breadcrumbs, the rest of the chervil, and top with knobs of butter. Bake in the oven for 35 minutes and serve piping hot.

Suggested wine pairing: a white Languedoc.

Sardines

The sardine season is from May to October. These fish have a very delicate flesh and they must be very fresh. Do not purchase sardines with loose scales, brown gills (they should be red), a strong odor, or a body that isn't shiny and firm.

Sardines can be found in abundance along the Atlantic coast, from the south of England to the south of Morocco. They are also fished in the Mediterranean Sea.

Barbecued sardines are delicious, but they need to be cooked fast so they do not burn (2 minutes per side is sufficient). To reduce the smell when cooking, remove the heads, gut, clean, and rub with a bay leaf. Sardine fillets can also be prepared on a griddle, in a frying pan, in the oven, or marinated.

Serves 4

- 6 large, fresh sardines (or 12 defrosted fillets)
- 1 orange
- 8 sprigs of flat-leaf parsley
- 1 large onion
- 2 anchovy fillets in oil
- 10 cL (½ cup) olive oil
- 2 dessert spoons (1¼ Tbsp) pine nuts
- 2 dessert spoons (1¼ Tbsp) raisins
- 6 dessert spoons (4 Tbsp) breadcrumbs
- salt
- pepper
- 6 bay leaves

Italian-style stuffed sardines

Chic
Preparation: 20 min
Cooking time: 20 min

Rinse and remove the heads from the sardines. Using a small, sharp knife carefully slit the underside down the middle (without completely separating in two), and remove the backbone. Grate half of the orange zest and juice the pulp. Finely chop the parsley. Peel and chop the onion and cut the anchovy fillets into small pieces.

Preheat the oven to 200°C (400°F) (th. 6/7). Pour half of the oil into a frying pan and sauté the onion for 5 minutes. Add the anchovies, pine nuts, raisins, and breadcrumbs. Stir for 7 minutes over low heat. Remove from the heat and add the parsley, zest, salt, and pepper.

Place the sardines (skin facedown) in an oiled ovenproof dish. Spread the filling over the fish and lay the bay leaves on top. Add the rest of the oil and the orange juice. Bake in the oven for 4 to 5 minutes and serve warm.

Suggested wine pairing: a dry Bergerac (South West France).

Mackerel with a white wine sauce

Classic

Preparation: 30 min – Cooking time: 25 min – Chilling time: 24 h

Serves 4

- 8 small mackerel
- 3 onions
- 4 shallots
- 2 carrots
- 40 cL (1¾ cups) dry white wine
- 15 cL (⅔ cup) white wine vinegar
- 1 bunch mixed herbs
- 1 clove
- 1 dessert spoon (2 tsp) cilantro seeds
- 2 organic lemons
- salt
- pepper

Ask your fishmonger to gut, clean, and remove the heads from the mackerel. Rinse and pat them dry. Peel the onions, shallots, and carrots. Cut the carrots into round slices and finely chop the shallots and onions.

Place the onions, shallots, and carrots in a saucepan with the wine, vinegar, mixed herbs, clove, and cilantro seeds. Add 1 L (4 cups) of water, bring to a boil then reduce the heat, partially cover, and simmer for 20 minutes.

Wash and cut the lemons into thin, round slices. Place in a casserole dish and add the fish, salt, and pepper. Pour the boiling marinade into the dish and leave to simmer for 4 to 5 minutes, depending on the size of the mackerel.

Cool the mackerel in the dish, then transfer to a deep dish with the juice and marinate for 24 hours in the refrigerator. Take the dish out of the refrigerator 30 minutes before serving, and serve with toasted farmhouse bread and salted butter.

Suggested wine pairing: a Sèvre et Maine Muscadet.

Grilled mackerel fillets & avocado sauce

Inventive

Preparation: 20 min – Cooking time: 6 min

Serves 4

- 2 organic limes
- 4 mackerel fillets
- salt
- 2 avocados
- ½ red onion
- 8 sprigs of cilantro
- Tabasco sauce, a few drops

Wash and dry the limes. Finely grate the zest of one lime, and then juice both limes. Place the mackerel fillets in a deep dish and make several slits in the skin. Add the salt and half of the lime juice, reserving the other half for later.

Heat a cast iron grill. Peel, pit, and cut the avocados into tiny cubes. Place them in a mixing bowl with the lime zest and remaining juice. Finely chop the red onion and the cilantro leaves, and add to the mixing bowl. Add salt and a few drops of Tabasco sauce, stir gently and place in the refrigerator.

Place the mackerel fillets, skin-side down, on the hot grill for 4 minutes, turning over carefully. Turn off the heat and leave to cook for another 2 minutes.

Serve the mackerel piping hot with the cold avocado sauce. White rice is an ideal side dish.

Suggested wine pairing: a white Touraine sauvignon.

Spaghetti with queen scallops, garlic flakes & pecorino cheese

Chic

Preparation: 30 min
Cooking time: 15 min

Serves 4

- 10 garlic cloves • 150 g (5 oz) peppered pecorino
- 1 ficelle de pain (a thin baguette)
- 6 dessert spoons (4 Tbsp) olive oil • 400 g (14 oz) spaghetti
- 500 g (1 lb) queen scallops (fresh or defrosted)
- salt • pepper

Peel and shred the garlic. Grate the pecorino. Slice the bread into croutons. In a frying pan, heat 4 dessert spoons (2¾ Tbsp) of oil and fry the garlic for 1 minute. Remove the garlic and place on a paper towel. Sauté the croutons in the same garlic oil.

Cook the spaghetti in a stew pot filled with boiling salted water for 8 to 11 minutes (depending on the cooking instructions). Meanwhile, cook the scallops with the rest of the olive oil in a large frying pan over a high heat for 3 to 4 minutes. Season with salt and pepper.

Quickly drain the spaghetti and transfer to a mixing bowl. Immediately stir in the scallops and their juice. Transfer the spaghetti to four deep bowls. Sprinkle with the croutons and the garlic and serve with the grated cheese.

Suggested wine pairing: a white Saumur (Loire Valley).

Cod with mustard & tomato

Informal
Preparation : 15 min
Cooking time : 15 min

Serves 4

- 20 g (³⁄₄ oz) butter
- 4 dessert spoons (2³⁄₄ Tbsp) finely chopped shallots (fresh or frozen)
- 4 dessert spoons (2³⁄₄ Tbsp) mustard
- 4 thick cod steaks (about 120 g / 4¹⁄₄ oz each)
- salt • pepper • 1 small can peeled tomatoes
- 3 dessert spoons (2 Tbsp) dry white wine
- 4 dessert spoons (2³⁄₄ Tbsp) olive oil
- 4 dessert spoons (2³⁄₄ Tbsp) breadcrumbs
- 2 dessert spoons (1¹⁄₄ Tbsp) finely chopped parsley (fresh or frozen)

Preheat the oven to 180°C (350ºF) (th 6). Butter an ovenproof dish and add the shallots. Spread the mustard over the cod steaks. Add salt and pepper, and lay the fish on top of the shallots.

Pour the canned tomatoes over the fish. Drizzle with the white wine and half of the oil. Sprinkle with breadcrumbs and bake in the oven for 15 minutes.

When cooked, drizzle with the rest of the oil, sprinkle with parsley, and serve directly from the dish. Serve with bouillon-cooked fresh coconut, rice, or mashed potatoes.

Suggested wine pairing: a white Graves (Bordeaux).

- 2 chicken bouillon cubes
- 2 onions
- 80 g (2¾ oz) butter
- 250 g (8¾ oz) risotto rice
  (arborio or carnaroli)
- salt
- pepper
- 10 cL (½ cup) dry white wine
- 200 g (7 oz) crabmeat
  (canned or defrosted)
- 1 slice of Parmesan
  (50 g / 1¾ oz)

Crab risotto

Chic

Preparation: 20 min – Cooking time: 30 min

Dilute the bouillon cubes in 1 L (4 cups) of boiling water and keep warm. Peel and finely chop the onions. Melt 50 g (1¾ oz) of butter in a casserole dish. Cook the onions and stir for 10 minutes until they are soft. Add the rice and continue stirring for 2 minutes so that it is well coated in butter. Add the salt, pepper, and wine. Stir until the liquid has evaporated.

Add the hot bouillon, cover, and cook for 18 minutes over medium heat. Meanwhile, grate the Parmesan and flake the drained crabmeat. When only 1 cm (½ inch) of bouillon is left in the dish, turn off the heat and stir in the rest of the butter and the Parmesan. Allow to settle for 2 minutes.

Place the risotto in a hot serving dish. Sprinkle with the crab and serve immediately.

CVF recommendation: For a spicy flavor, peel and chop 3 cm (1½ inches) of fresh ginger and cook with the onions.

Suggested wine pairing: a white Alsace pinot.

Sautéed prawns with mango juice

Exotic

Preparation: 30 min
Cooking time: 2 min

Serves 4

- 20 large uncooked prawns (defrosted or fresh) • 1 mango
- ½ dessert spoon (1 tsp) sherry vinegar
- 1 dessert spoon (2 tsp) olive oil
- salt • pepper
- 30 cilantro leaves

Shell the prawns. Peel the mango, remove the pit, and mix the pulp with a blender (or a food processor). Add the vinegar and 1 to 2 dessert spoons (2 tsp to 1¼ Tbsp) of water and continue to blend until the mixture is smooth and creamy.

In a frying pan, heat the oil. Salt and pepper the prawns and sauté them over high heat for 1 minute on each side. Remove from the heat and add the cilantro leaves.

Pour the mango juice into four soup bowls. Add 5 prawns to each bowl, sprinkle with the cilantro leaves, and serve.

CVF recommendation: When shelling the prawns, use a cocktail stick to remove the black thread along the spine, which can give them a bitter taste.

Suggested wine pairing: a dry Montlouis sur Loire.

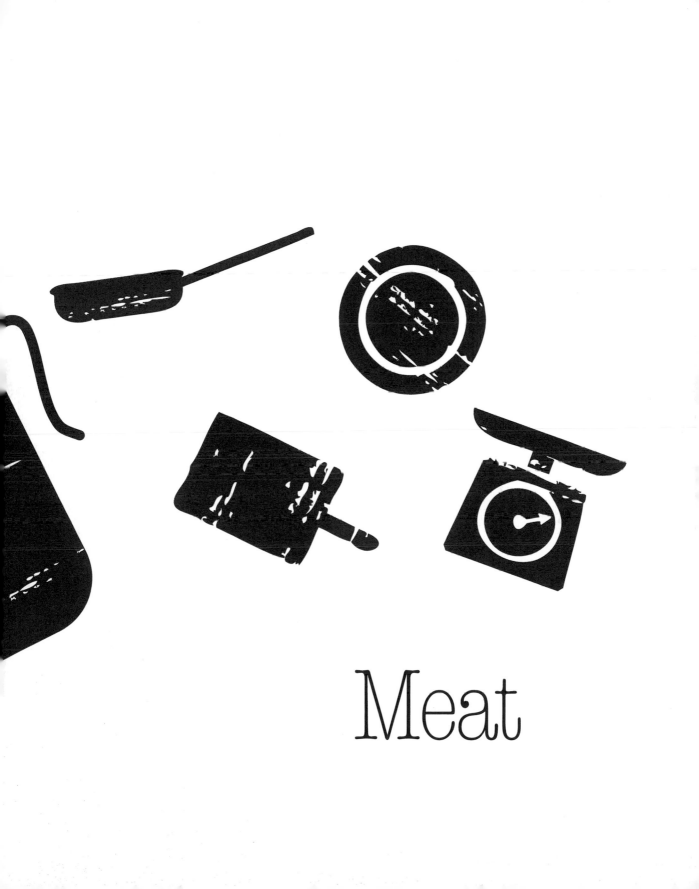

Meat

Stuffed chicken surprise

Informal
Preparation: 15 min
Cooking time: 25 min

Serves 4

- 4 chicken breasts • 20 g ($^3/_4$ oz) butter • salt
- freshly ground pepper • 2 thin slices boiled ham
- 4 slices sheep's milk cheese (Ossau-iraty)
- 2 dessert spoons ($1^1/_4$ Tbsp) finely chopped parsley (fresh, dried, or frozen)
- 1 chicken bouillon cube

Preheat the oven to 180°C (350ºF) (th. 6). Halve the chicken breasts lengthwise but do not separate them completely.

Melt the butter in a large frying pan. Quickly sear the chicken breasts on both sides over high heat until they change color. Remove from the pan and season with salt and pepper.

Place half a slice of ham, a slice of cheese, and some parsley in the middle of each breast and close by squeezing the edges of the chicken.

Place the chicken breasts in an ovenproof dish. Crumble the bouillon cube and sprinkle overtop. Add 15 cL ($^2/_3$ cup) of water and bake in the oven for 15 minutes. Baste from time to time.

Serve piping hot with mashed potatoes or a lamb's lettuce salad.

CVF recommendation: You can replace the boiled ham with a thin slice of cured ham and the sheep's milk cheese with Swiss cheese.

Suggested wine pairing: a red Touraine (Loire Valley).

How to choose a leg of lamb

The leg of lamb, the hind leg, is a high-quality cut of meat. It was given the name gigot in French because of its shape, which is similar to that of an old musical instrument called the gigue. A whole leg of lamb includes the saddle (or the two loins with the hip). Otherwise, it is a half leg of lamb. A leg of lamb weighing 1.5 kg (3 lb) is ideal for 6 people. A joint that is short and round will be tastier than a long, thin one. If you like your meat rare, the recommended cooking time is 15 minutes to the pound in a hot oven (210°C / 410°F / th. 7). However, if it is boned and stuffed, it will need to be cooked longer. The "Gigot de Sept Heures" (a leg of lamb that is slow-cooked for seven hours until it is tender enough to just fall off the bone) is a very famous and popular French dish. Lamb lovers are also very fond of lamb shanks, a very tender cut of lamb that comes from the upper part of the leg.

Serves 6

- 1 leg of lamb (about 1.3 kg / 2¾ lb)
- 60 g (2 oz) salted, shelled pistachios
- 2 dessert spoons (1¼ Tbsp) honey
- 100 g (3½ oz) butter
- 12 soft dried apricots
- 2 sprigs of rosemary
- salt
- pepper

Roast leg of lamb with pistachios & soft apricots

Chic

Preparation: 20 min – Cooking time: 50 min

Preheat the oven to 180°C (350°F) (th. 6). Using a small, sharp knife, cut some small slits in the lamb and push the pistachios into the slits. Rub the lamb with 50 g (1¾ oz) of butter and season with salt and pepper. Place the lamb in an ovenproof dish and roast for 50 minutes.

After about 30 minutes, prepare the garnish. Pour the honey into a small ovenproof dish. Add the knobs of butter, apricots, and rosemary leaves. Cover with a sheet of tinfoil and bake in the oven for 15 minutes. Pour the mixture over the lamb, and leave to cook for another 5 minutes.

When the lamb is cooked, switch off the oven and cover the dish with tinfoil. Leave it in the oven with the door ajar for 10 minutes.

Place the leg of lamb and the garnish on a warm serving dish. Pour 10 cL (½ cup) of boiling water into the oven dish and using a spatula, scrape the drippings off the bottom of the dish. Strain the sauce and pour into a gravy boat.

Suggested wine pairing: a Saint-Julien (a red Bordeaux, Médoc wine).

Serves 4

- 1 slice of white sandwich bread (without the crust)
- ½ bunch cilantro
- 4 merguez sausages (spicy sausage)
- 200 g (7 oz) minced beef
- 1 egg
- salt
- pepper
- 2 dessert spoons (1¼ Tbsp) cornstarch
- 10 cL (½ cup) vegetable oil

For the salad:

- 10 cL (½ cup) vegetable oil
- 500 g (1 lb) baby carrots
- 3 garlic cloves
- ¼ dessert spoon (1 tsp) ground cumin
- 10 cL (½ cup) olive oil
- salt
- pepper

Spicy meatball shish kebabs with carrot & cumin salad

Exotic

Preparation: 40 min – Cooking time: 35 min

Soak four wooden skewers in water (to prevent them from sticking to the food and from burning while cooking). Crumble the bread in a bowl of water, and then remove and wring out excess water. Finely chop the cilantro. Remove the skin from the sausages and put them in a mixing bowl with the minced beef, cilantro, egg, bread, salt, and pepper. Knead until the texture is smooth and shape into meatballs.

Roll the meatballs in the cornstarch. Cook in a frying pan with the oil for 10 minutes, turning regularly. Remove from the pan and pat dry with a paper towel. Thread three meatballs onto each skewer

Peel and cut the carrots into 1-cm (½ inch) thick round slices. Peel and finely chop the garlic and sauté in a frying pan with the olive oil. Add 75 cL (3¼ cups) of hot water and bring to the boil. Add the carrots, cumin, salt, and pepper. Cook for another 20 minutes, or until the liquid has evaporated.

Switch on the broiler. Place the shish kebabs in an ovenproof dish and broil for 5 minutes (turning once). Serve with the warm carrot salad.

Suggested wine pairing: a Côte de Brouilly (a red Beaujolais).

Serves 6

- 1 oxtail cut into small pieces
- 1 dessert spoon (2 tsp) oil
- 1 bunch mixed herbs
- 1 clove
- 5 cL (¼ cup) brandy
- 25 cL (1 cup) red wine
- 1 dessert spoon (2 tsp) veal bouillon powder
- 1 bunch flat-leaf parsley
- salt
- pepper

For the mashed potatoes:

- 300 g (10 oz) potatoes
- 600 g (1¼ lb) sweet potatoes
- 50 g (1¾ oz) butter
- 3 dessert spoons (2 Tbsp) heavy cream (35%)
- 225 g (8 oz) breadcrumbs

Cottage pie with sweet potatoes

Informal

Preparation: 40 min – Cooking time: 1 h 30 min

In a pressure cooker, sauté the oxtail in hot oil for 5 minutes. Add the mixed herbs, clove, brandy, wine, 1 L (4 cups) of water, and the veal bouillon powder and stir. Cover and cook for 45 minutes. Once cooked, leave to stand for 15 to 20 minutes. Remove the lid, drain the meat, and then shred it with a fork into a mixing bowl. Stir in 20 cL (¾ cup) of skimmed gravy, the chopped parsley, salt, and pepper and set aside.

Preheat the oven to 180°C (350°F) (th. 6). Peel and rinse the potatoes and sweet potatoes. Transfer to a saucepan with cold, salted water and cook for 25 minutes. Drain the potatoes and blend with a food mill. Add the butter and cream and mix well. Season with salt and pepper.

Spread out the oxtail pieces in a gratin dish. Cover the meat with the mashed potatoes, sprinkle with breadcrumbs, and oven bake for 15 to 20 minutes or until golden brown. Serve in the gratin dish with a green salad as a side dish.

CVF recommendation: If using a stew pot instead of a pressure cooker, cook for 1½ hours over low heat.

Suggested wine pairing: a red Bergerac (South West France).

How to cook different cuts of veal

Grill / fry / roast: chuck, sweetbread, liver, plate, round, thick rib, brisket, hanger steak, cutlet, chop.

Braise: chuck, thick rib, brisket, plate, shank, hanger steak, round, chop.

Boil: chuck, thick rib, plate, shank, hanger steak, brisket.

Serves 4

- 1 kg (2¼ lb) plate of veal cut into 120 g (4¼ oz) pieces
- 2 dessert spoons (1¼ Tbsp) oil
- 50 g (1⅜ oz) butter
- 15 cL (⅔ cup) dry white wine
- juice of 1 lemon
- 1 dessert spoon (2 tsp) veal bouillon powder
- 1 bunch mixed herbs
- 8 carrots
- 1 bunch small white scallions
- 1 dessert spoon (2 tsp) liquid honey
- 1 dessert spoon (2 tsp) cumin seeds
- salt
- pepper
- 1 bunch flat-leaf parsley

Plate of veal with caramelized carrots

Convivial
Preparation: 30 min – Cooking time: 2 h

Heat the oil in a casserole dish, add the veal, and brown on each side. Drain the veal and discard the oil. Place the dish back on the heat with a knob of butter. Add the wine, lemon juice, bouillon powder, 20 cL (¾ cup) of hot water, and the mixed herbs. Stir well and add the veal. Season with salt and pepper, cover, and leave to simmer for 2 hours.

Meanwhile, peel the carrots and, if they are big, cut them into medium-sized pieces. Peel the scallions. Melt the rest of the butter in a frying pan. Add the carrots, scallions, honey, cumin, and 10 cL (½ cup) of water. Season with salt and pepper, stir, and cover. Simmer over low heat for 30 minutes, stirring from time to time.

Finely chop the parsley. Drain the meat and transfer to a serving dish. Arrange the vegetables around the meat, coat with the sauce, sprinkle with the parsley, and serve.

CVF recommendation: Ask your butcher for some veal spare ribs, which are rare, tasty cuts of veal that are delicious with this recipe.

Suggested wine pairing: a Chinon (a Loire Valley red).

Serves 4

- ½ spicy chorizo
- 1 garlic clove
- 1 onion
- ½ bunch flat-leaf parsley
- 2 pork tenderloin fillets
- 2 dessert spoons (1¼ Tbsp) olive oil
- 5 cL (¼ cup) dry white wine
- salt
- pepper

Pork tenderloin with chorizo

Chic

Preparation: 35 min – Cooking time: 35 min

Remove the skin from the chorizo and cut into cubes. Place the chorizo in a frying pan and leave to sweat over low heat until crisp. Drain the cubes on a paper towel. Meanwhile, peel and finely chop the garlic and onion. Rinse the parsley, remove the leaves, pat dry, and finely chop.

Place the fillets on the worktop and slit lengthwise. In a bowl, combine the chorizo and the parsley and season with salt. Spoon this mixture into the fillets and fold. Tie them together with kitchen string, without squeezing them too tightly.

Heat the oil in a casserole dish. Sauté the garlic and onion until soft but not brown. Once cooked, drain in a skimmer. Sear the fillets in the same casserole dish over high heat. Reduce the heat. Add the garlic, onion, wine, and season with a little salt and pepper (not too much because of the chorizo). Cover and leave to simmer for 25 minutes. Serve the pork tenderloin fillets hot. Mashed potatoes make an ideal side dish.

Suggested wine pairing: a red Côtes du Rhône Villages Cairanne.

Serves 4

- 1 dessert spoon (2 tsp) vinegar
- 3 dessert spoons (2 Tbsp) oil
- salt
- freshly ground pepper
- 8 eggs
- 30 g (1 oz) butter
- 200 g (7 oz) finely chopped onions
- 500 g (1 lb) black sausage (boudin noir)
- 2 dessert spoons (1¼ Tbsp) finely chopped parsley
- 1 bunch curly endive lettuce

Black sausage omelet

Economical

Preparation: 10 min – Cooking time: 20 min

Using a fork, combine the vinegar and oil with the salt and pepper in a salad bowl. Add the lettuce, toss, and set aside.

Break the eggs into a mixing bowl and beat with a fork. Melt the butter in a large, non-stick frying pan and sauté the onions for 5 minutes. Remove the skin from the sausage and cut into thin, round slices. Add to the pan and brown for 10 minutes over high heat, stirring regularly. Sprinkle with half the parsley, stir, and add the eggs.

When the omelet is cooked (soft and moist but not dry), slide it onto a serving dish. Sprinkle with the rest of the parsley and serve piping hot with the salad.

Suggested wine pairing: a Touraine Gamay (a Loire Valley red).

Tandoori rack of lamb

Original
Preparation: 40 min – Marinade: 12 h
Cooking time: 30 min

Serves 4

- 1 can (400 g / 14 oz) coconut milk
- 50 g (1¾ oz) tandoori spice mix
- 1 rack of lamb with 8 chops • salt • 50 g (1¾ oz) butter
- 1 kg (2¼ lb) sweet potatoes • ½ bunch cilantro • pepper

To accompany the dish:
- 1 jar of mango chutney (homemade or store bought)

About 12 hours in advance, hand whisk the coconut milk with the tandoori spice mix. Place the rack of lamb in an ovenproof dish, season with salt, and brush with the tandoori mixture. Cover with plastic wrap and leave to marinate in the refrigerator for 12 hours.

When 12 hours is up, peel and cut the sweet potatoes into pieces. Boil for 25 to 30 minutes then crush with a fork (or a potato masher). Add the butter and the freshly chopped cilantro. Season with salt and pepper.

At the same time, preheat the oven to 180°C (350°F) (th. 6). Place the rack of lamb in its marinade in the oven and bake for 25 to 30 minutes depending on how you like your meat (rare, medium, or well done). Baste regularly with the marinade while cooking. The skin should be red and crispy.

Once cooked, remove from the oven. Cover the dish with two sheets of tinfoil and leave to stand for 15 minutes. Strain the sauce and pour into a gravy boat. Serve with the mashed sweet potatoes and the mango chutney.

Suggested wine pairing: a red Minervois la Livinière (Languedoc).

Serves 4

- 1 pork tenderloin
- juice of 1 lemon
- 4 dessert spoons (2¾ Tbsp) olive oil
- 1 dessert spoon (2 tsp) oregano
- salt
- pepper
- 1 bunch sage
- 12 cherry tomatoes
- 200 g (7 oz) spicy or mild chorizo

Pork & chorizo shish kebabs with sage

A summer favorite
Preparation: 20 min
Cooking time: 12 min

Soak eight wooden skewers in water (to prevent them from sticking to the food and from burning while cooking). Cut the pork tenderloin into cubes and place in a salad bowl with the lemon juice, oil, and oregano. Season with salt and pepper, stir, and leave to marinate.

Meanwhile, remove the leaves from the sage. Wash and dry the cherry tomatoes and halve the largest ones.

Cut the chorizo into large pieces. Remove the skin and cut into 1-cm (½ inch) thick, round slices.

Drain the wooden skewers. Thread the ingredients onto the skewers, alternating between a cube of meat, sage leaves, slices of chorizo, and cherry tomatoes.

Cook on a barbecue or a hot, cast iron grill for 12 minutes, turning regularly. Serve hot.

Suggested wine pairing: a red Ventoux (Rhône Valley).

Serves 4

- 1 eggplant
- 2 zucchinis
- 500 g (1 lb) small, firm potatoes (Charlotte or Roseval variety)
- 2 carrots
- 3 garlic cloves
- 1 onion
- 800 g (1¾ lb) pork tenderloin
- 2 dessert spoons (1¼ Tbsp) oil
- 2 level dessert spoons (1¼ Tbsp) colombo curry powder (a Caribbean spice mixture)
- salt
- pepper
- 1 small pepper
- juice of 1 lime

Pork colombo with vegetables

Convivial

Preparation: 30 min
Cooking time: 1 h 40 min

Wash the eggplant and the zucchinis and cut into large cubes. Peel, wash, and halve the potatoes. Peel the carrots and cut into 3-cm (1¼ inch) thick pieces. Peel and chop the garlic and onion. Cut the meat into medium-sized pieces.

Pour the oil into a casserole dish and brown the meat for 5 minutes over high heat. Add the onion and garlic and sauté for 3 minutes. Add the colombo curry powder, salt, and pepper. Place all the vegetables in the casserole dish and cover with sufficient water. Place the lid on the casserole dish and leave to cook over medium heat for an hour.

Add the chopped pepper and leave to cook for another 30 minutes. Just before serving, add the lime juice, stir, and serve piping hot.

Suggested wine pairing: a red Crozes-Hermitage (Rhône Valley).

meat **113**

Sweet & sour lamb shanks with garlic

Classic

Preparation : 30 min
Cooking time : 2 h

Serves 4

- 1 bunch fresh thyme • 1 bunch rosemary
- 2 dessert spoons (1¼ Tbsp) liquid honey
- 3 dessert spoons (2 Tbsp) olive oil • 4 lamb shanks
- 10 cL (½ cup) sweet wine (type muscat) • 20 garlic cloves
- 600 g (1¼ lb) potatoes (Ratte variety)
- 30 g (1 oz) butter • salt • pepper

Preheat the oven to 160°C (325°F) (th. 5/6). Crumble the thyme and the rosemary in a bowl. Add the honey and stir. Heat the oil in a casserole dish and brown the lamb shanks. Season with salt and pepper. Add the honey and herb mixture and caramelize lightly over low heat. Add the wine and 20 cL (¾ cup) of water.

Cover and bake in the oven for 2 hours. Turn the meat several times while cooking and baste often with the juice. Add the garlic (unpeeled) halfway through the cooking process.

Meanwhile, brush the potatoes under slow, running water. Place them in a stew pot with cold, salted water and cook for 15 minutes after the water has come to a boil. Drain and sauté in a frying pan with the butter. Season with salt and pepper.

Drain the lamb shanks and keep warm. Reduce the cooking juices for several minutes over high heat until the liquid thickens. Serve the lamb shanks with the garlic cloves, sautéed potatoes, and gravy.

Suggested wine pairing: a Saint-Émilion Grand Cru (a red Bordeaux).

Peking duck & sauerkraut

Original
Preparation: 20 min
Cooking time: 20 min

Serves 4

• 2 duck breasts • 2 dessert spoons (1¼ Tbsp) liquid honey
• 10 cL (½ cup) soy sauce • salt • pepper
• 650 g (1¼ lb) cooked sauerkraut

Preheat the oven to 180°C (350°F) (th. 6). Using a sharp knife, make crisscross slits in the fatty part of the duck breasts. Place the duck breasts, fat side down, in a hot frying pan and sear over high heat for 5 minutes. (Be careful not to burn yourself with the splattering hot fat).

Meanwhile, pour the honey and soy sauce into a small saucepan. Heat over low heat and stir until the mixture thickens. Place the duck breasts in an ovenproof dish (without the fatty juices). Season with salt and pepper and add the honey and soy sauce mixture. Bake in the oven for 10 to 15 minutes. Heat the sauerkraut in a casserole dish.

Remove the duck breasts from the oven and cover with two sheets of tinfoil. Leave to stand for 7 to 8 minutes and slice.

Transfer the sauerkraut to a serving dish. Lay the duck breast slices on top and coat with the sauce. Serve immediately.

Suggested wine pairing: an Alsace pinot noir.

Vegetarian

- 500 g (1 lb) button mushrooms
- 2 shallots
- 2 dessert spoons (1¼ Tbsp) whole-grain mustard
- 10 cL (½ cup) table cream (18%)
- 1 dessert spoon (2 tsp) paprika
- 1 bunch flat-leaf parsley
- 350 g (12¼ oz) stortini pasta
- 40 g (1½ oz) butter
- 2 dessert spoons (1¼ Tbsp) brandy
- salt
- pepper

Mushroom Stroganoff

Convivial

Preparation: 30 min
Cooking time: 20 min

Remove the stalks from the mushrooms. Rinse, dry well, and cut the cap into thin slices. Peel and finely chop the shallots. Combine the mustard, cream, and paprika in a bowl. Finely chop the parsley.

Cook the pasta in boiling, salted water for about 8 minutes, depending on the brand. Meanwhile, in a large frying pan, lightly sauté the shallots in the butter for 5 minutes until they are soft but not brown. Add the mushrooms and increase the heat so they brown.

When all the water has evaporated, pour the heated brandy into the pan and flambé.

Drain the pasta and add to the frying pan with the mustard, cream, and paprika mixture. Season the pasta with salt and pepper, and stir over low heat for 5 minutes. Sprinkle with parsley and serve immediately.

Suggested wine pairing: an Alsace pinot noir.

Serves 6

- 300 g (10 oz) pumpkin flesh
- 2 onions
- 60 g (2 oz) soft butter
- 3 eggs
- 100 g (3½ oz) flour
- 1 sachet (11 g / ¼ oz) baking powder
- 30 g (1 oz) walnut kernels
- 75 g (2⅔ oz) grated Comté cheese
- 2 dessert spoons (1¼ Tbsp) olive oil
- salt
- freshly ground pepper

Cheese & pumpkin cake

Welcoming
Preparation: 20 min – Cooking time: 45 min

Preheat the oven to 210°C (410°F) (th. 7). Cut the pumpkin flesh into cubes and cook in a saucepan with boiling, salted water for 20 minutes. Drain and purée with a blender. Peel and finely chop the onions and sauté for about 10 minutes, stirring regularly.

In a mixing bowl, combine the butter and the eggs. Add the flour, baking powder, pumpkin purée, onions, crushed walnuts, and grated Comté cheese. Season with salt and pepper and stir well until the mixture is smooth and creamy. Using a brush, oil a cake pan with the rest of the oil, and pour in the mixture (it should fill two-thirds of the cake pan). Bake in the oven for 35 to 40 minutes. Eat warm with a green salad.

Suggested wine pairing: a white Côtes du Jura.

Serves 6

- 20 g (¾ oz) butter (for the cake pan)
- 1 small bunch mint
- 100 g (3½ oz) feta cheese
- 2 zucchinis
- 10 cL (½ cup) olive oil + 2 dessert spoons (1¼ Tbsp)
- 3 eggs
- 10 cL (½ cup) milk
- 180 g (6½ oz) flour
- 1 sachet (11 g / ¼ oz) baking powder
- 100 g (3½ oz) grated Parmesan
- 20 g (¾ oz) pine nuts
- salt
- pepper

Zucchini & feta cake

A Summer Favorite
Preparation: 15 min – Cooking time: 50 min

Preheat the oven to 180°C (350°F) (th. 6). Line a cake pan with buttered parchment paper (unless you are using a silicone pan). Rinse, pat dry, and finely chop the mint. Dice the feta cheese.

Wash and wipe the zucchinis. Discard the ends and dice. In a frying pan, heat two dessert spoons (1¼ Tbsp) of oil and sauté the zucchinis over high heat for 5 minutes.

Break the eggs into a mixing bowl and beat lightly with 10 cL (½ cup) of oil and the milk. Stir continuously while adding the flour, baking powder, feta, Parmesan, diced zucchinis, mint, and three quarters of the pine nuts. Season with salt and pepper and stir again until the mixture is smooth and creamy.

Pour the mixture into the cake pan and sprinkle with the remaining pine nuts. Bake for about 45 minutes. Use a skewer or a knife to check the cooking process. If the blade comes out clean, the cake is cooked.

Allow the cake to cool before removing it from the cake pan and cut into slices or cubes.

Suggested wine pairing: a white Corsican wine.

Matching pasta with the right sauce

Long, thin pasta, such as spaghetti, spaghettini, and linguine: liquid sauce; creamy sauce; mushroom or seafood sauce; pesto; oil, garlic, and pepper sauce; bolognese sauce; tuna and tomato sauce; and egg-based sauces, such as carbonara.

Long, wide, and thick pasta, such as tagliatelle, mafaldine, and pappardelle: tomato sauce; bolognese sauce; cheese sauce; and seafood or shellfish sauce.

Short-cut, twisted, ribbed pasta, or orecchiette pasta: thick, rich sauce that clings to the pasta; sauce with tiny pieces of meat or vegetables; and ricotta sauce.

Spinach-stuffed pasta: vegetable sauce.

Squid ink pasta: fish or seafood sauce.

Serves 6

- 1 onion
- 30 g (1 oz) butter
- 3 dessert spoons (2 Tbsp) olive oil
- salt
- pepper
- 1 fresh red chili pepper, seeded
- 1 pinch superfine (berry) sugar
- 1 large can peeled tomatoes
- 500 g (1 lb) spaghetti
- 100 g (3½ oz) pecorino cheese or grated Parmesan

Spaghetti with tomato & chili pepper

Economical
Preparation: 15 min – Cooking time: 20 min

Peel and finely chop the onion. Heat the butter and oil in a frying pan and sauté the onions until they are soft. Season with salt and pepper. Add the seeded pepper, pinch of sugar, and peeled tomatoes with their juice. Cook for 15 minutes, while breaking up the tomatoes with a fork.

Meanwhile, bring salted water to the boil in a stew pot. Add the spaghetti and cook for 10 to 12 minutes (depending on the package instructions).

When the spaghetti is cooked, drain and transfer to a large salad bowl. Coat with sauce and sprinkle with grated cheese. Do not mix before serving so the pasta absorbs the sauce gradually, making it much tastier!

Suggested wine pairing: a Barbera d'Asti (a red from Piedmont, Italy).

Grilled vegetable sandwiches

A quick bite
Preparation : 15 min
Cooking time : 5 min

Serves 4

- 600 g (1½ lb) frozen grilled vegetables (defrosted)
- 8 slices of multi-grain sandwich bread • 1 jar of pesto
- pepper • 50 g (1¾ oz) freshly grated Parmesan
- 1 dessert spoon (2 tsp) lemon juice • 3 dessert spoons (2 Tbsp) olive oil
- salt • 50 g (1¾ oz) pre-washed, ready-to-use arugula

Preheat the oven to 180°C (350°F) (th. 6). Gently pat dry the defrosted, grilled vegetables with a paper towel and slice them into two or three large pieces. Remove the crust from the bread. Spread the pesto over the 8 slices of bread. Divide the vegetables evenly over four of the slices, add pepper, and sprinkle with Parmesan. Place the remaining slices on top, with the pesto facing the vegetables.

Bake in the oven for about 5 minutes, or until the bread is lightly toasted. Meanwhile, prepare the vinaigrette. Using a fork, combine the lemon juice, oil, salt, and pepper in a salad bowl. Add the arugula and toss. Cut the hot sandwiches into triangles and serve with the salad.

Suggested wine pairing: a white Cheverny (Loire Valley).

Serves 4

- 3 zucchinis
- 3 eggplants
- 10 cL (⅓ cup) olive oil
- salt
- pepper
- 1 onion
- 2 garlic cloves
- 30 cL (1¼ cups) tomato coulis (in a jar)
- 1 dessert spoon (2 tsp) dried oregano
- 400 g (14 oz) lasagna sheets
- 250 g (8¾ oz) mozzarella

Grilled vegetable lasagna

Informal

Preparation : 30 min
Cooking time : 45 min

Preheat the oven to 180°C (350°F) (th. 6). Wash the zucchinis and the eggplants. Remove the ends and cut into ½-cm (¼ inch) thick, round slices. Brush both sides of each slice with oil and place on a cast iron grill.

Grill 1 minute per side (a few at a time) and season with salt and pepper. Peel and finely chop the onion and garlic. Sauté in a saucepan with 2 dessert spoons (1¼ Tbsp) of oil until they are soft. Add the tomato coulis and oregano, season with salt and pepper, and reduce over low heat for 10 minutes.

Oil an ovenproof dish. Alternate the lasagna sheets, grilled vegetables, and tomato coulis and finish with a layer of lasagna sheets. Finely slice the mozzarella and lay over the lasagne. Bake in the oven for 30 minutes and serve piping hot.

Suggested wine pairing: a Côtes de Provence rosé.

White, purple, and green asparagus

Asparagus is white if it is grown entirely in the soil, with no light. Asparagus has pinkish-purple tips if it has been exposed to sunlight. Asparagus is green when it grows above the ground because photosynthesis occurs.

Green asparagus is the most slender and tender. It does not need to be peeled and can be sautéd in a pan. White asparagus needs to be peeled with a vegetable peeler from the top of the stalk to the bottom.

Asparagus can be steamed or cooked in boiling water. It will stay fresh for two or three days in a damp dish towel at the bottom of the refrigerator. Kept longer, it becomes stringy.

Serves 4

- 24 green asparagus spears
- 2 garlic cloves
- 120 g (4¼ oz) butter
- 5 dessert spoons (¼ cup) balsamic vinegar
- salt
- pepper

Sautéed asparagus in balsamic butter

Light
Preparation: 15 min – Cooking time: 10 min

Brush, rinse, and gently pat dry the asparagus. Halve it lengthwise. Peel and finely chop the garlic.

Melt a knob of butter in a large frying pan. Cook the garlic for about 3 minutes or until it is soft. Add the vinegar, the remaining butter, and 4 dessert spoons (2¾ Tbsp) of water. Stir for 2 minutes over medium heat.

Place the asparagus in the frying pan and, stirring continuously, cook for about 5 minutes until tender. Add salt (very little) and pepper. Transfer the asparagus to the serving plates, coat with the balsamic butter, and serve immediately.

CVF recommendation: For this recipe, use exclusively green asparagus, which is ideal for this cooking method.

Suggested wine pairing: a white Saint Joseph (Rhône Valley).

Goat cheese, mint & raisin cake

Convivial
Preparation : 10 min
Cooking time : 45 min

Serves 6

• 60 g (2 oz) raisins • 200 g (7 oz) soft, fresh goat cheese (Petit Billy)
• 10 mint leaves, finely chopped • 100 g (3½ oz) grated Comté cheese
• salt • freshly ground pepper

For the batter:
• 3 large eggs • 220 g (8 oz) flour • 1 sachet (11 g / ¼ oz) baking powder
• 10 cL (½ cup) milk • 10 cL (½ cup) olive oil
• salt • freshly ground pepper

Preheat the oven to 180°C (350°F) (th. 6) and line a cake pan with parchment paper. Place the raisins in a small saucepan with a little water and cook over a high heat until the water has evaporated.

Prepare the batter. Using an electric whisk or a food processor, whisk the eggs with the flour, baking powder, oil, milk, salt, and pepper in a mixing bowl.

Roughly break up the goat cheese and add to the batter. Add the finely chopped mint, raisins, grated Comté cheese, and, eventually, a little salt and pepper. Slowly combine the ingredients and pour into a cake pan. Bake in the oven for 45 minutes. Serve either warm or cold.

CVF recommendation: Use an electric knife to prevent the cake from crumbling and cut into fairly large slices.

Suggested wine pairing: a white Menetou-Salon (Loire Valley).

Different types of risotto rice

Any risotto dish needs a specific type of Italian rice with a high starch content, which enables it to absorb liquids. Properly cooked risotto is rich and creamy and, at the same time, al dente.

The arborio and carnaroli varieties are the most well-known and are easy to find. Vialone nano is another excellent variety, which is also very popular but more difficult to find.

The average amount of risotto rice per person is 70 g (2½ oz).

Hints & tips

Serves 4 to 6

- 100 g (3⅛ oz) arugula
- 2 garlic cloves
- 1 bunch basil
- 1 bunch flat-leaf parsley
- 1 bunch tarragon
- 40 g (1½ oz) freshly grated Parmesan
- 1 dessert spoon (2 tsp) pine nuts
- 2 chicken bouillon cubes
- 1 onion
- 30 g (1 oz) butter
- 300 g (10 oz) risotto rice (arborio or carnaroli)
- 15 cL (⅔ cup) dry white wine
- 150 g (5 oz) mascarpone cheese
- salt
- pepper

Risotto verde with mascarpone

Chic
Preparation : 30 min – Cooking time : 25 min

Prepare, wash, and spin-dry the arugula. Blanch for 1 minute in boiling, salted water and drain well. Peel the garlic. Rinse, pat dry, and finely chop the herbs. Blend the herbs, arugula, garlic, Parmesan, and pine nuts in a food processor and set aside.

Dilute the bouillon cubes in 1.2 L (5 cups) of boiling water. Peel and finely chop the onion. Melt the butter in a stew pot, add the onion, and cook for 5 minutes while stirring. Add the risotto rice and stir with a spatula until it is translucent. Pour in the wine and stir for 1 minute before adding the hot bouillon. Season with salt and pepper. Cover, reduce the heat, and leave to simmer for 18 minutes.

When cooked, add the herb mixture and the mascarpone. Stir briskly with a spatula. Cover, leave to stand for 3 to 5 minutes, and serve.

Suggested wine pairing: a white Alsace pinot.

Eggplant fans with goat cheese

Classic

Preparation: 30 min
Cooking time: 1 h

Serves 6

• 6 long eggplants • 4 round, ripe tomatoes • 2 large sweet onions
• 150 g (5 oz) goat cheese in the form of a log (type sainte-maure-de-touraine)
• 15 cL (⅔ cup) olive oil • salt • pepper
• 100 g (3½ oz) black olives • 6 sprigs of fresh thyme

Preheat the oven to 210°C (410°F) (th. 7). Wash and dry the eggplants. Cut into slices lengthwise but do not separate them completely because each slice must remain attached to the stalk so the eggplants are fan-shaped.

Cut the tomatoes into ½-cm (¼ inch) thick, round slices. Peel and cut the onions into ½-cm (¼ inch) thick, round slices. Cut the cheese into round slivers. Insert the tomato, onion, and cheese slices between the eggplant slices.

Oil an ovenproof dish. Place the eggplant fans in the dish and season with salt and pepper. Add the olives and sprinkle with thyme. Pour the remaining oil over the eggplants and place in the oven. Bake for 15 minutes then reduce the temperature to 150°C (300°F) (th. 5). Bake for another 45 minutes and serve hot, warm, or cold.

Suggested wine pairing: a red Lirac (Rhône Valley).

(Photo page 134)

Pappardelle with arugula & orange sauce

Flavorful

Preparation: 20 min
Cooking time: 10 min

Serves 4

- 2 organic oranges • 500 g (1 lb) pappardelle (or tagliatelle)
- 50 g (1¾ oz) arugula • 30 cL (½ cup) light cream (10%)
- salt • freshly ground pepper

Wash and dry the oranges. Peel the zest of one orange and cut it into very thin strips. Blanch the zest: place the strips in a small saucepan and cover with cold water. Bring to a boil, drain, and repeat the operation twice (to remove the bitterness).

Finely grate half the zest of the second orange. Cook the pasta in a stew pot filled with boiling, salted water for 8 to 10 minutes, depending on the brand.

Meanwhile, coarsely chop the arugula. Heat the cream in a small saucepan and add the arugula and grated zest. Season with salt and pepper. When it starts boiling, remove from the heat and mix.

Drain the pasta and transfer to a hot dish. Coat with the arugula sauce, mix, and sprinkle with the zest. Serve immediately.

Suggested wine pairing: a white Languedoc.

(Photo page 135)

Serves 4

- 350 g (12¼ oz) spaghetti
- 100 g (3½ oz) frozen green beans
- 300 g (10 oz) canned tuna fish in brine
- 1 small jar sun-dried tomatoes in oil
- salt
- pepper
- 1 dessert spoon (2 tsp) lemon juice
- 2 dessert spoons (1¼ Tbsp) olive oil
- 2 dessert spoons (1¼ Tbsp) black pitted olives
- 2 dessert spoons (1¼ Tbsp) capers
- 1 small bunch basil

Mediterranean style spaghetti

Informal

Preparation: 15 min
Cooking time: 20 min

Cook the spaghetti in a large quantity of boiling, salted water for about 10 minutes, depending on the cooking instructions.

In another saucepan, cook the beans for 12 minutes in boiling, salted water. Meanwhile, place the tuna in a sieve, pat dry, and flake with a fork. Drain the tomatoes and cut into thin strips. Set aside two dessert spoons (1¼ Tbsp) of their oil.

In a bowl, combine the salt, pepper, lemon juice, olive oil, and the oil of the tomatoes. Drain the spaghetti and the beans and transfer to a large, warm salad dish. Add the tuna, olives, tomatoes, capers, and sauce and mix. Chop the basil at the last minute and sprinkle over the spaghetti before serving.

Suggested wine pairing: a Coteaux d'Aix en Provence rosé.

Serves 4

- 1 shallot
- 1 curly endive lettuce
- 1 dessert spoon (2 tsp) balsamic vinegar
- 3 dessert spoons (2 Tbsp) oil
- salt
- pepper
- 50 g (1¾ oz) walnut kernels
- 8 eggs
- 25 g (1 oz) butter
- 125 g (4½ oz) Roquefort cheese
- 1½ dessert spoons (1 Tbsp) heavy cream (35%)

Roquefort cheese omelette

Informal

Preparation: 20 min
Cooking time: 10 min

Peel and finely chop the shallot. Wash and dry the lettuce. In a bowl, prepare the vinaigrette with the chopped shallot, vinegar, oil, salt, and pepper. Briefly dry roast the walnuts in a frying pan and set aside.

Break 4 eggs into a mixing bowl. Separate the white from the yolk of the 4 other eggs. Add the yolks to the mixing bowl with the other eggs. Beat the egg whites until stiff. Add the crumbled Roquefort and the cream to the ingredients in the mixing bowl. Season with pepper and mix gently with a fork. Scoop up the mixture, gradually fold in the egg whites, turn the bowl a little and repeat the operation several times.

Melt the butter in a large frying pan. Add the Roquefort and egg mixture and evenly cook over a low heat for 7 to 8 minutes. The omelet should be soft and moist.

Toss the lettuce with the vinaigrette in a salad dish. Sprinkle with the roasted nuts. Transfer the omelet to a serving dish and serve immediately with the salad.

Suggested wine pairing: a sparkling Montlouis (Loire Valley).

Desserts

How to melt chocolate

The success of a chocolate dessert depends largely on the melting process. If chocolate is melted too quickly, it is lumpy and difficult to work with.

The best way to melt chocolate is to place it in a heat-resistant bowl over a saucepan of hot water. Break or chop the chocolate into small squares. Make sure the water bubbles but does not boil over into the bowl. Stir regularly with a plastic spatula until the texture is smooth. When three-quarters of the chocolate has melted, remove it from the heat and continue stirring.

If you use a microwave oven, switch it off every 20 seconds and stir the chocolate. Continue until it has melted completely.

For about 30 squares:

- 350 g (12¼ oz) dark chocolate
- 100 g (3½ oz) icing sugar
- 200 g (7 oz) sweetened condensed milk
- 100 g (3½ oz) butter
- 220 g (8 oz) shredded coconut
- ½ dessert spoon (1 tsp) oil

Chocolate & coconut fondants

Chic

Preparation : 20 min – Cooking time : 10 min – Chilling time : 1 h

Oil a rectangular dish (about 30 × 20 cm / 12 × 8 inches). Break the chocolate into small squares and melt in a heat resistant bowl over a saucepan of hot water. Pour the chocolate into the dish and place in the refrigerator so it hardens.

Meanwhile, blend the icing sugar, condensed milk, soft butter, and coconut in a bowl, preferably using an electric whisk, until the mixture is smooth and creamy.

When the chocolate is hard, pour the coconut mixture into the dish. Smooth with a spatula and return the dish to the refrigerator until the mixture hardens.

Remove from the dish, with the coconut layer facing upward. Cut into squares with a large knife and serve cold.

Suggested pairing: a single malt whisky.

- 1 small can sliced pineapple in its juice
- 1 vanilla pod
- 20 g ($\frac{3}{4}$ oz) butter
- 50 g ($1\frac{3}{4}$ oz) superfine (berry) sugar
- 12 butter cookies (try Traou Mad de Pont-Aven)
- 40 cL ($1\frac{3}{4}$ cups) vanilla ice cream

Mini pineapple tarts

Express

Preparation: 15 min
Cooking time: 10 min

Drain the slices of pineapple and cut into small triangles. Split the vanilla pod lengthwise and scrape out the seeds with the tip of a knife.

In a frying pan, melt the butter. Add the pineapple triangles, sugar, and vanilla seeds. Caramelize over a medium heat while carefully and regularly turning over the pineapple.

Place the butter cookies onto serving dishes and cover each cookie with the pineapple triangles. Pour the caramel from the frying pan over the top and serve immediately with a scoop of vanilla ice cream.

Suggested wine pairing: a white Crémant du Jura.

Coffee & walnut cake

Serves 6

- 150 g (5 oz) walnut kernels
- 3 eggs
- 200 g (7 oz) superfine (berry) sugar
- ½ sachet (5½ g / ⅛ oz) baking powder
- 250 g (8¾ oz) flour
- 180 g (6½ oz) soft, salted butter
- 2 dessert spoons (1¼ Tbsp) coffee extract

Welcoming

Preparation: 15 min – Cooking time: 40 min

Preheat the oven to 160°C (325°F) (th. 5-6) and line a cake pan (18 to 20 cm / 7 to 8 inches in length) with parchment paper buttered on both sides. Place in the refrigerator.

Lightly pan roast the walnuts in a frying pan and set aside. Blend the eggs, 150 g (5 oz) of the sugar, and the baking powder in a food processor. Slowly and carefully, add the soft butter, flour, and coffee extract, and continue blending until the mixture is smooth and creamy. Add 100 g (3½ oz) of coarsely crushed walnuts and stir with a spatula. Pour the batter into the cake pan and bake in the oven for 40 minutes.

Meanwhile, prepare the caramel by melting the rest of the sugar in a small saucepan. Remove from the heat and add the remaining 50 g (1¾ oz) of walnuts. Once they are coated in the caramel, remove from the saucepan one by one and place on a sheet of parchment paper.

Remove the cake from the pan and place on an oven rack to cool. Carefully remove the caramelized walnuts from the parchment paper and place on top of the cake.

Suggested wine pairing: a vin de paille (a Jura straw wine).

Chocolate & biscoff marquise

Serves 6

- 350 g (12¼ oz) dark chocolate (at least 52% of cocoa)
- 200 g (7 oz) biscoff cookies (coffee-flavored shortbread)
- 80 g (2¾ oz) butter
- 30 cL (1¼ cups) heavy cream (35%)
- 1 large pinch cinnamon

Prepare in advance

Preparation: 20 min – Chilling time: 6 h – Cooking time: 40 min

Coarsely cut the chocolate into small squares with a knife. Using your fingers, break up the cookies into small pieces, but not powder. Cut the butter into small cubes. Line a small cake pan with plastic wrap (or parchment paper).

Pour the cream into a saucepan. Add the butter and bring slowly to a boil. Add the chocolate and stir over a low heat with a spatula until the mixture is smooth and creamy. Add the cinnamon and cookies and stir.

Pour the chocolate and biscoff mixture into the cake pan and leave to cool. Place in the refrigerator for at least 6 hours. When it is time to serve, remove the marquise from the cake pan and slice. Serve cold with custard or a scoop of vanilla ice cream.

Suggested pairing: an XO brandy.

Figs with almond cream

Classic

Preparation: 10 min – Cooking time: 30 min

Serves 6

- 125 g soft butter (4½ oz) + 20 g (¾ oz) for the ramekins
- 6 large or 12 small figs
- 4 eggs
- 100 g (3½ oz) icing sugar
- 125 g (4½ oz) ground almonds
- 2 dessert spoons (1¼ Tbsp) rum
- 2 dessert spoons (1¼ Tbsp) flaked almonds
- 1 dessert spoon (2 tsp) superfine (berry) sugar
- 125 g (4½ oz) red currants

Preheat the oven to 180°C (350°F) (th. 6). Butter six ovenproof ramekins. Wash and dry the figs. Cut the figs into quarters and place in the ramekins.

Using a food processor, combine the eggs, butter, icing sugar, ground almonds, and rum. When the mixture is smooth and creamy, pour it over the figs and sprinkle with the flaked almonds. Bake in the oven for about 25 minutes.

Meanwhile, in a saucepan, add the superfine (berry) sugar to 10 cL (½ cup) of water and bring to a boil. Add the stemmed red currants and leave to simmer for 5 minutes. Strain the juice trough a fine sieve and leave to cool. Coat the warm figs and cream with a little red currant sauce and serve.

Suggested wine pairing: a naturally sweet Rivesaltes Ambré.

Apricot & almond gratin

A summer favorite

Preparation: 15 min – Cooking time: 40 min

Serves 6

- 100 g (3½ oz) butter
- 1 kg (2⅓ lb) apricots (frozen)
- 100 g (3½ oz) superfine (berry) sugar
- 100 g (3½ oz) ground almonds
- 1 egg
- 8 small macaroons (amaretti)

Preheat the oven to 180°C (350°F) (th. 6). Melt a knob of butter in a frying pan. Add the apricots (frozen), and sprinkle with 2 dessert spoons (1¼ Tbsp) of sugar. Stirring continuously, sauté over high heat until all the water has evaporated. Transfer to a buttered, ovenproof dish.

Melt the remaining butter in a small saucepan and leave to cool. In a mixing bowl, blend the rest of the sugar, the ground almonds, and the melted butter. Add the egg and blend until the mixture is smooth and creamy.

Coat the apricots with the almond cream and bake in the oven for 20 minutes, or until the cream starts to brown. Coarsely crumble the macaroons. Remove the dish from the oven and sprinkle with the macaroon crumble. Return the dish to the oven for 5 to 10 minutes. Leave to cool a little and serve warm.

Suggested wine pairing: a naturally sweet Beaumes-de-Venise muscat (Rhône Valley).

- ½ organic lemon
- 1 level dessert spoon (2 tsp) cornstarch
- 6 eggs
- 500 g (1 lb) fromage blanc (French-style fresh cheese) with 30% fat content
- 120 g (4¼ oz) superfine (berry) sugar
- salt
- 6 dessert spoons (4 Tbsp) heavy cream (35%)
- 1 vanilla pod
- 230 g (8 oz) shortcrust pastry (homemade or ready-made)

Fromage blanc tart

Informal

Preparation: 20 min
Cooking time: 35 min

Finely grate the zest of the half lemon and squeeze the juice. Mix the lemon juice and the cornstarch in a bowl. Separate the egg whites from the yolks.

Place the yolks, fromage blanc, sugar, grated zest, diluted corn starch, pinch of salt, heavy cream, and vanilla seeds in a mixing bowl. Preferably using an electric whisk, mix the ingredients.

Preheat the oven to 180°C (350ºF) (th. 6). Line a tart dish with the shortcrust dough and prick with a fork. Beat the egg whites until stiff. Slowly fold the egg whites into the fromage blanc and fill the tart dish with this mixture.

Bake in the oven for 15 minutes then leave the oven door ajar for 5 minutes to let the steam out. Close the door and bake for another 20 minutes. Remove the tart from the oven and leave to cool on an oven rack. Serve at room temperature.

Suggested wine pairing: a sweet Vouvray Moelleux (Loire Valley).

Shortcrust pastry recipe

- 100 g (3½ oz) superfine (berry) sugar • salt • 1 egg
- 250 g flour (8¾ oz) • 1 sachet (11 g / ¼ oz) of vanilla sugar
- 125 g (4½ oz) butter

Mix the sugar, salt, and egg in a bowl. Add the flour and vanilla sugar. Rub the dough with your fingertips until the mixture resembles breadcrumbs. Add the knobs of butter and quickly knead until the dough is evenly bound.

You can use brown sugar instead of superfine (berry) sugar and you can replace ⅕ of the flour with the same volume of ground almonds. You can also reduce the amount of sugar if the topping is very sweet.

Serves 4

- 1 sheet of shortcrust pastry (homemade or ready-made)
- 50 g (1¾ oz) butter + 10 g (⅓ oz) for the tart dish
- 2 eggs
- 75 g (2⅔ oz) superfine (berry) sugar
- 2 sachets (22 g / ¾ oz) vanilla sugar
- 2 dessert spoons (1¼ Tbsp) liquid honey
- 40 g (1½ oz) cornstarch
- 150 g (5 oz) walnuts and a few kernels
- salt

Walnut tart

Prepare in advance

Preparation: 20 min – Cooking time: 30 min

Preheat the oven to 210°C (410°F) (th. 7). Roll out the shortcrust pastry and place it in a buttered tart dish. Reserve some kernels for the topping and crush the rest. Melt the butter in the microwave or a saucepan. Separate the egg whites from the yolks. Place the yolks in a mixing bowl with the superfine (berry) and vanilla sugars and the honey. Blend with a hand whisk until the mixture turns white. Add the cornstarch, the melted butter, and the crushed walnuts.

Add a pinch of salt to the egg whites and beat until stiff, then slowly fold into the walnut mixture with a metal spoon. Pour the mixture over the pastry and top with the walnut kernels. Bake in the oven for 30 minutes and serve warm.

Suggested wine pairing: a naturally sweet Maury (Roussillon).

Pear & walnut crumble

Chic

Preparation : 30 min – Cooking time : 25 min

Serves 4

- 50 g (1⅜ oz) butter
- 4 ripe pears
- 50 g (1⅜ oz) walnuts
- 2 dessert spoons (1¼ Tbsp) brown sugar
- 2 dessert spoons (1¼ Tbsp) flour
- 2 dessert spoons (1¼ Tbsp) shredded coconut

Remove the butter from the refrigerator and soften at room temperature. Preheat the oven to 180°C (350°F) (th. 6). Leaving the skin and stems on the pears, wash and dry them. Crush the walnuts. In a bowl, mix the walnuts with the sugar, flour, shredded coconut, and 40 g (1½ oz) of soft butter. Rub the mixture using your fingertips until it crumbles.

Slice the pears in three horizontally. Place the bottom slices in a buttered, ovenproof dish (if necessary, cut off the rounded part so that the slice sits flat). Sprinkle with some crumble, add the second pear slice, and repeat. Place the third slice on top of the crumble and bake in the oven for 25 minutes, or until the pears are golden and the crumble is crispy. Serve warm with custard or a pear sorbet.

Suggested wine pairing: a Jurançon (a sweet dessert wine from South West France).

CVF recommendation : If the pears are very firm, poach them in 50 cL (2 cups) of water and 200 g (7 oz) of sugar for 10 minutes.

The pear, a seasonal fruit

Summer pears: French Bartlett, Williams (Bartlett). These sweet, juicy pears are harvested in August.

Fall pears: Beurre Hardy, Louise Bonne, and Comice.

Winter pears: Conference and Passe Crassane. These pears are harvested in the fall and kept in cold storage to be sold throughout the winter.

Serves 6

- 2 eggs
- 1 sheet of shortcrust pastry
- 50 g (1¾ oz) gingerbread
- 75 g (2⅔ oz) soft butter
- 75 g (2⅔ oz) superfine (berry) sugar
- 1 level dessert spoon (2 tsp) flaked almonds
- 10 cL light cream (10%)
- 4 ripe pears
- 2 dessert spoons (1¼ Tbsp) flaked almonds

Pear & gingerbread tart

Welcoming
Preparation: 25 min – Cooking time: 30 min

Separate the egg whites from the yolks. Place the pastry with its parchment paper in a tart dish. Prick the pastry with a fork and brush with the egg white. Place in the refrigerator.

Preheat the oven to 180°C (350°F) (th. 6). Break up the gingerbread into crumbs. In a mixing bowl, blend the butter, sugar, egg yolks, gingerbread, cornstarch, and cream until the mixture is smooth and creamy. Peel and quarter the pears and remove the seeds and cores.

Remove the tart dish from the refrigerator. Spread the gingerbread cream over the pastry. Place the quartered pears on top of the cream with the rounded sides facing upward. Bake in the oven for 25 to 30 minutes.

Meanwhile, briefly dry roast the flaked almonds in a frying pan and leave to cool. Sprinkle over the pears and serve the tart warm or cold.

Suggested wine pairingt: a sparkling Mauzac (Southwest France).

Serves 6

- 60 g (2 oz) candied ginger (can be found at most Asian grocery stores)
- 80 g (2¾ oz) dark chocolate (at least 52% cocoa)
- 15 cL (⅔ cup) table cream (18%)
- 1 egg yolk + 4 egg whites
- 20 g (¾ oz) superfine (berry) sugar

Chocolate mousse with candied ginger

Spicy

Preparation: 20 min
Cooking time: 10 min
Chilling time: 3 h

Cut the candied ginger into small cubes. Break the chocolate into small pieces and, without stirring, leave it to melt in a heat-resistant bowl over a saucepan of boiling water. Bring the cream to a boil. Remove the bowl of chocolate from the saucepan and add the cream. Stir until the mixture is smooth and leave it to cool. Add the egg yolk, sugar, and cubes of candied ginger. Stir well.

Whisk the egg whites until they are stiff. Fold a third of the egg whites into the chocolate mixture; then gently add in the remaining egg whites by scooping up the mixture and folding it over the egg whites until they are completely incorporated into the chocolate mixture.

Transfer the mousse to a serving bowl or to individual glass bowls and place in the refrigerator for 3 hours before serving.

Suggested pairing: Jamaican rum.

Apple pastillas with lightly salted butter

Chic

Preparation : 30 min
Cooking time : 10 min

Serves 6

- 20 walnut kernels • 5 Belle de Boskoop apples
- 125 g (4½ oz) lightly salted butter
- 100 g (3½ oz) superfine (berry) sugar
- pinch cinnamon • 8 sheets of phyllo pastry

Coarsely crush the walnuts. Peel the apples. Remove the seeds and the core and slice into 1-cm (½ inch) cubes. Preheat the oven to 180°C (350°F) (th. 6). Melt 75 g (2⅔ oz) of butter in a frying pan. Add the diced apple and 100 g (3½ oz) of sugar. Cook over high heat for 10 minutes, stirring regularly. Add the walnuts and the pinch of cinnamon. Set aside.

Melt the remaining 50 g (1¾ oz) of butter in a small saucepan. Place a sheet of phyllo pastry onto a baking tray and brush with butter. Place a second sheet on top and brush with butter. Repeat with two more sheets.

Spread the frying pan mixture over the pastry sheets, leaving a space of 3 cm (1¼ inches) between the mixture and the edge of the pastry. Fold the edges over the filling. Individually butter the 4 remaining pastry sheets, cover the filling, and fold the edges to shape the pastillas. Bake in the oven for about 10 minutes, or until the pastillas is golden brown. Serve immediately.

Suggested pairing: a dry farm cider.

(Photo page 160)

Red berry crumble

Quick

Preparation: 15 min
Cooking time: 35 min

Serves 6

- 125 g (4½ oz) red currants • 125 g (4½ oz) blueberries
- 125 g (4½ oz) blackberries • 125 g (4½ oz) raspberries
- 150 g (5 oz) superfine (berry) sugar • 125 g (4½ oz) cold butter
- 75 g (2⅔ oz) ground almonds • 100 g (3½ oz) flour
- 3 pinches ground cinnamon • 2 pinches salt

Preheat the oven to 210°C (410°F) (th. 7). Butter the base and sides of an ovenproof dish measuring about 25 cm (10 inches) in diameter.

Wash and stem the red currants. Place all the fruits in a mixing bowl and sprinkle with 50 g (1¾ oz) of sugar. Gently mix the fruits and sugar then transfer them to the ovenproof dish and spread out in an even, compact layer.

Slice the rest of the butter into small pieces and place them in a food processor. Add the remaining sugar, ground almonds, flour, cinnamon, and salt. Mix gradually so the mixture is crumbly.

Cover the fruit with the crumble and bake in the oven for 30 to 35 minutes until the crumble is golden. Serve hot or warm with crème fraîche (heavy sour cream) or custard.

Suggested wine pairing: a Pineau des Charentes rosé.

(Photo page 161)

Serves 6

For the pastry:
- 250 g (8¾ oz) flour
- 30 g (1 oz) ground almonds
- 125 g (4½ oz) butter
- 80 g (2¾ oz) icing sugar
- 1 egg
- pinch salt

For the filling:
- 3 unwaxed lemons
- 100 g (3½ oz) butter +
  1 knob for the tart dish
- 6 eggs
- 300 g (10 oz) superfine (berry)
  sugar

Lemon tart

Economical
Preparation: 20 min – Resting time (dough): 30 min
Cooking time: 25 min

Place the dough ingredients a little bit at a time in a food processor and mix slowly until the dough forms a ball. You can also hand mix the ingredients instead of using a food processor. Wrap the dough in plastic wrap and place in the refrigerator for 30 minutes.

Preheat the oven to 180°C (350°F) (th. 6). Wash the lemons, grate their zests, and juice the pulp. Melt the butter. Beat the eggs with the sugar, lemon juice, and grated zests and add the melted butter. Reserve.

Butter a tart dish. Roll out the dough and place it in the dish. Prick the dough with a fork and blind bake in the oven for 15 minutes. After 15 minutes, pour the lemon mixture over the pastry base and leave to bake for another 25 minutes (if you are making individual tartlets, only bake for another 15 minutes). Remove the tart from the oven and the tart dish and leave to cool on an oven rack. Serve cold.

Suggested wine pairing: a Jurançon (a sweet wine from South West France).

CVF recommendation: Cook some round slices of lemon in 20 cL (¾ cup) of water and 200 g (7 oz) of sugar for 25 minutes. Leave to cool and use to decorate the tart.

Serves 6

- 20 cL (¾ cup) very cold table cream (18%) or light cream (10%)
- 6 ripe peaches (preferably white)
- 1 dessert spoon (2 tsp) icing sugar
- 3 dessert spoons (2 Tbsp) flaked almonds
- 6 dessert spoons (4 Tbsp) red currant jelly
- ½ lemon
- ½ L (2 cups) vanilla ice cream

Peach melba

A summer favorite
Preparation: 30 min – Cooking time: 2 min

Place the table cream and the whisks of the mixer in the freezer for several minutes. Blanch the peaches by immersing them in a saucepan of boiling water for 30 seconds to loosen the skin, then drain and peel.

Halve the peaches, remove the pit, and place each half in a small, individual dish. Whip the cream until it thickens and becomes stiff. Fold the icing sugar into the firm, whipped cream. Dry roast the flaked almonds in a frying pan, turning regularly so they do not burn. Melt the red currant jelly in a small saucepan with the juice of half a lemon.

Add a scoop of vanilla ice cream to the peaches and coat with the melted jelly. Top with whipping cream (use a piping bag, if possible) and sprinkle with roasted almond flakes. Serve immediately.

Suggested wine pairing: a Vouvray demi-sec (Loire Valley).

Pear & verbena delight

Light
Preparation : 15 min
Cooking time : 5 min
Chilling time : 2 h

Serves 4

- 6 dessert spoons (4 Tbsp) apple and pear compote (homemade or ready-made)
- 2 pears (Conference variety)
- 50 g (1¾ oz) cane sugar
- 2 dessert spoons (1¼ Tbsp) dried verbena
- 1 bunch mint • 2 g (1 tsp) agar-agar or 2 sheets of gelatin

Place 1 dessert spoon (2 tsp) of compote in 4 small glasses. Peel the pears, remove the seeds, and cut into cubes. In a saucepan, bring 30 cL (1¼ cups) of water to a simmer with the sugar, diced pears, verbena, and half of the mint and cook for 5 minutes.

Remove from the heat and leave to infuse for another 5 minutes. Strain the mixture and add the agar-agar. Bring to the boil and stir for 1 minute. Return the diced pears to the saucepan and add the rest of the chopped mint. Pour the mixture into the small glasses. Leave to cool and then place in the refrigerator for about 2 hours. Serve cold.

CVF recommendation: If using gelatin, soften the sheets in cold water first and then squeeze to remove the excess water. Off the heat, melt them in the boiling, filtered juice before adding the diced pears.

Suggested pairing: Brut Champagne.

Types of butter

Raw butter: made from raw, unpasteurized cream. It has a very rich flavor but a short shelf life.

Beurre extra fin (extra fine butter): a French classification of butter. This butter must be made within 72 hours of the milk being collected. After the cream has been skimmed off the milk, the pasteurization and churning have to be done within 48 hours. The use of frozen cream is illegal for extra fine butter, but for "beurre fin" (fine butter), 30% of the cream used can be previously frozen.

Low-fat butter and light butter: made from low-fat pasteurized cream. Some types have additives like cornstarch. Low-fat butter contains 60% to 65% milk fat, whereas "light" butter contains between 39% and 41%. These types can be cooked at very low temperatures, but they are not ideal for cooking due to their high water content.

Unsalted butter: obtained after the cream has been churned.

Salted butter: contains 3% salt, usually table salt. However, some salted butters contain sea salt crystals, which add a little crunch!

Lightly salted butter: contains between 0.5% and 3% table salt or salt crystals.

Organic butter: comes from the milk of cows that have been raised in accordance with organic farming rules and regulations.

- 50 g (1¾ oz) soft slightly salted butter
- 400 g (14 oz) prunes
- 5 eggs
- 130 g (4½ oz) superfine (berry) sugar
- 1 sachet (11 g / ¼ oz) vanilla sugar
- 220 g (7¾ oz) flour
- 75 cL (3¼ cups) whole milk

Prune custard flan with salted butter

Regional

Preparation : 20 min
Cooking time : 30 min

Preheat the oven to 180°C (350°F) (th. 6), butter a springform pan, and pit the prunes. Break the eggs into a mixing bowl and add both sugars. Preferably using an electric whisk, mix the ingredients while slowly adding the flour, then the milk, and, finally, half of the remaining butter. Whisk until the mixture is smooth.

Place the prunes in the buttered springform pan and pour the mixture over the top. Bake in the oven for about 30 minutes. Five minutes before the end of the baking process, slice the remaining butter into small pieces and place on top of the flan. Cook for the remaining five minutes, and then insert a knife into the flan. If the blade comes out clean, the flan is cooked. Leave to cool before serving.

Suggested wine pairing: a white Pineau des Charentes.

Nutella fondant tart

Informal

Preparation: 20 min
Chilling time: 30 min
Cooking time: 20 min

Serves 6 to 8

For the pastry:
- 100 g (3½ oz) butter
- 50 g (1¾ oz) icing sugar
- 30 g (1 oz) ground almonds
- 1 pinch salt
- 1 egg
- 200 g (7 oz) flour

For the filling:
- 200 g (7 oz) dark chocolate (more than 52% cocoa)
- 100 g (3½ oz) butter
- 200 g (7 oz) Nutella
- 20 g (¾ oz) superfine (berry) sugar
- 1 egg + 2 yolks

Prepare the pastry. Melt the butter and pour it into a mixing bowl with the icing sugar, ground almonds, salt, egg, and flour. Combine the ingredients by rubbing with your fingertips until the dough is crumbly. Form a ball and wrap it in plastic wrap. Place the dough in the refrigerator for at least 30 minutes.

Once the dough has chilled, preheat the oven to 150°C (300°F) (th. 5). Roll out the dough, without working it too much, and place it in a tart dish. Cover the base with parchment paper and dried beans and blind bake in the oven for 10 minutes. Remove the dish from the oven and discard the paper and beans.

Melt the chocolate and the butter in the microwave or in a heat-resistant bowl over boiling water. Then, combine the Nutella, sugar, egg, yolks, chocolate, and butter in a bowl until the mixture is smooth. Pour over the pastry base and bake in the oven at 180° (350°F) (th. 6) for 10 to 12 minutes. Serve warm.

Suggested wine pairing: a sparkling Crémant du Jura.

Banana & Nutella tartlets

Economical

Preparation: 20 min
Cooking time: 15 min

Serves 4

- 1 sheet of puff pastry
- 2 bananas
- 20 g (¾ oz) butter
- 50 g (1¾ oz) superfine (berry) sugar
- 4 dessert spoons (2¾ Tbsp) Nutella
- sea salt

Preheat the oven to 210°C (410°F) (th. 7). Line four mini tart pans with the puff pastry. Prick the base with a fork. Blind bake for about 10 minutes then leave to cool.

Cut the bananas into round slices and brown in a frying pan with the butter and sugar. Fill the tartlets with the bananas, coat with a layer of Nutella and sprinkle with a little sea salt. Serve at room temperature.

Suggested pairing: an amber rum.

Coffee panna cotta

Chic

Preparation: 20 min
Cooking time: 10 min
Chilling time: 4 h

Serves 6

- 3 sheets of gelatin (3 × 2 g / 0.1 × 0.07 oz) • 30 cL (1¼ cups) whole milk
- 50 cL (2 cups) table cream (18%) • 80 g (2¾ oz) superfine (berry) sugar
- 2 dessert spoons (1¼ Tbsp) liquid coffee extract

For the cream:
- 25 cL (1 cup) milk • 1 star anise • 2 egg yolks
- 40 g (1½ oz) granulated sugar • ¼ dessert spoon (½ tsp) cornstarch
- a few drops coffee extract

Soften the gelatin in a bowl of cold water. In a saucepan, bring the milk, cream, sugar, and coffee extract to a boil for 3 minutes and then remove from the heat. Squeeze the gelatin to remove the excess water and add to the saucepan while stirring. You can prepare the panna cotta in silicone baking cups (such as Flexipan) or directly in six small bowls or wine glasses. Spoon the mixture into whatever you are using, allow it to cool, and then place in the refrigerator for at least 4 hours.

Prepare the cream. In a saucepan, heat the milk and the star anise. Cover and leave to infuse for 5 minutes. In a mixing bowl, beat the egg yolks and the sugar until the mixture turns white. Stirring gently, add the cornstarch, and slowly pour in half of the hot milk (without the star anise).

Pour this mixture into the saucepan containing the rest of the milk and place over medium heat (do not boil) until the cream thickens and coats the spatula. Remove from the heat and leave to cool. Add the coffee extract and place in the refrigerator. Serve the panna cotta cold with the cream in a separate bowl.

Suggested wine pairing: a naturally sweet Rasteau (Rhône Valley).

Serves 6

- 140 g (5 oz) soft butter +
  15 g (½ oz) for the tart dish
- 140 g (5 oz) superfine (berry)
  sugar
- 280 g (9¾ oz) flour +
  30 g (1 oz) flour for the
  worktop
- ½ dessert spoon (1 tsp) ground
  cinnamon
- 140 g (5 oz) ground almonds
- 1 level dessert spoon (2 tsp)
  cocoa powder
- 2 egg yolks
- salt
- 350 g (12¼ oz) raspberry jam

Linzer Torte

Regional

Preparation: 30 min
Resting time: 1 h
Cooking time: 45 min

Prepare the pastry. Slowly combine the soft butter and the sugar in a food processor. Continue mixing while gradually adding the flour, cinnamon, ground almonds, cocoa, egg yolks, and a pinch of salt. Shape the dough into a ball and wrap in plastic wrap. Place in the refrigerator for at least 1 hour.

After an hour, lightly butter a tart dish measuring 28 cm (11 inches) in diameter and take the dough out of the refrigerator. Shape a ball using three quarters of the dough and spread it in the dish with the palm of your hand. Cover with an even layer of jam.

Preheat the oven to 180°C (350°F) (th. 6). Sprinkle the worktop with flour and roll out the rest of the dough. Preferably using a fluted pastry wheel, cut out strips of dough measuring 1 cm (½ inch) wide. Lay out the strips in a lattice pattern over the jam. Pinch the ends so that the strips adhere to the rim.

Bake in the oven for about 45 minutes, or until the pastry is golden brown. Remove the tart from the oven and its dish and leave to cool on an oven rack.

Suggested wine pairing: a naturally sweet Maury (Roussillon).

Serves 4

- 200 g (7 oz) mascarpone
- 1 sheet of shortcrust pastry
- 500 g (1 lb) small strawberries
- 3 dessert spoons (2 Tbsp) mint liqueur (Get 27 or Menthe Pastille)
- 4 dessert spoons (2¾ Tbsp) icing sugar

Strawberry & mint tartlets

Quick

Preparation: 20 min – Cooking time: 15 min

Take the mascarpone out of the refrigerator in advance so it is soft. Preheat the oven to 180°C (350°F) (th. 6). Roll out the dough and, using a bowl turned upside down, divide it into four circles. Place the circles in four mini tart pans lined with parchment paper. Prick the base with a fork and bake in the oven for 12 to 15 minutes, until the pastry is golden brown.

In a mixing bowl, whisk the mascarpone with 2 dessert spoons (1¼ Tbsp) of icing sugar and the mint liqueur. Reserve in the refrigerator. Rinse the strawberries and halve or quarter, depending on their size. Remove the tartlets from the oven and the mini tart pans and leave to cool on an oven rack.

Just before serving, add the mascarpone and top with the sliced strawberries with the tip pointing upward. Decorate with sieved icing sugar and serve immediately.

Suggested wine pairing: a Vouvray (a sweet Loire Valley wine).

CVF recommendation: Sprinkle the tartlets with shelled, unsalted, coarsely crushed pistachios.

Serves 6

- 1 organic orange
- 1 organic lemon
- 1 vanilla pod
- 1 sprig rosemary
- ¼ dessert spoon (½ tsp) black peppercorns
- 1 cinnamon stick
- 1 L (4 cups) whole milk
- 150 g (5 oz) bomba rice
- 2 drops of bitter almond extract
- 100 g (3½ oz) superfine (berry) sugar
- 300 g (10 oz) Gariguette strawberries
- icing sugar

Spicy strawberry rice pudding

Flavorful

Preparation: 30 min – Cooking time: 45 min

Wash and dry the orange and lemon. Using a vegetable peeler, remove the zests without the pith. Split the vanilla pod lengthwise and scrape out the seeds with the tip of a knife. Place the vanilla pod and its seeds, rosemary, pepper, cinnamon, and zests in a muslin drawstring bag. Pour the milk into a saucepan, add the muslin bag and bring to a boil. Add the rice and almond extract.

Bring to a simmer, but not boil, stirring regularly every 5 minutes. After 30 minutes, stir in the superfine (berry) sugar. After another 15 minutes, when the rice is cooked, remove the muslin bag. Transfer the rice to a deep dish and leave to cool at room temperature.

Wash the strawberries, remove their stems, and halve. Just before serving, arrange the strawberries on top of the rice (similar to a tart) and sprinkle with icing sugar.

Suggested wine pairing: an Alsace gewürztraminer.

Pear & almond cream spring rolls

Chic

Preparation: 25 min
Cooking time: 10 min

Serves 4

- 100 g (3½ oz) soft butter • 1 egg yolk
- 70 g (2½ oz) superfine (berry) sugar • 70 g (2½ oz) ground almonds
- 8 halved pears (canned) • 4 sheets of phyllo pastry

Preheat the oven to 180°C (350°F) (th. 6). Reserve 30 g (1 oz) of butter for spreading over the spring rolls. Put the rest of the butter in a mixing bowl with the egg yolk, sugar, and ground almonds. Mix well until smooth and creamy.

Using a paper towel, carefully dry the pears and cut them into cubes. Spread the almond cream over half of each pastry sheet but leave the edges clear. Place the diced pears in the center, fold the long sides of the sheet inward and shape into spring rolls.

Transfer the spring rolls to a baking tray lined with parchment paper. Brush the spring rolls with the rest of the butter and bake in the oven for 8 to 10 minutes until golden. Serve the spring rolls hot with a scoop of almond milk ice cream or pear sorbet.

Suggested wine pairing: a Coteaux du Layon (a sweet Loire Valley wine).

Serves 4

- 100 g (3½ oz) flour
- 80 g (2¾ oz) + 30 g (1 oz) butter
- 120 g (4¼ oz) + 1 dessert spoon (2 tsp) superfine (berry) sugar
- 1 egg
- 1 dessert spoon (2 tsp) milk
- 8 fresh figs
- icing sugar
- 50 g (1¾ oz) shelled, unsalted pistachios

Fig & pistachio tart

Classic

Preparation: 10 min
Resting time: 30 min
Cooking time: 25 min

Preheat the oven to 180°C (350ºF) (th. 6). Put the flour, butter, and 20 g (¾ oz) of superfine (berry) sugar in a food processor and mix until the dough is crumbly. Add the egg and milk and mix very slowly until the dough forms a ball. Wrap the dough in plastic wrap and place in the refrigerator for 30 minutes.

Roll out the dough and line a tart dish. Prick the base with a fork. Wash, dry, and quarter the figs and spread them over the tart. Add some knobs of butter, sprinkle with icing sugar, and bake in the oven for 25 minutes.

Once baked, remove the tart from the oven and the tart dish and leave to cool on an oven rack. Caramelize the pistachios with 1 dessert spoon (2 tsp) of sugar in a non-stick frying pan on low heat, stirring frequently. Leave to cool, then coarsely crush. Before serving, sprinkle the tart with the pistachios and some icing sugar.

Suggested wine pairing: a Maury (a naturally sweet Roussillon wine).

Index

A

Alsatian griess soup _____ 22
Apricot & almond gratin _____ 150
Apple pastillas with lightly salted butter _____ 162
Arugula cigars _____ 13

B

Bacon, apple & prune quiche _____ 62
Banana & Nutella tartlets _____ 170
Black sausage omelet _____ 106

C

Cabecou parcels with a leek fondue & button
mushroom carpaccio _____ 13
Cheese & pumpkin cake _____ 122
Chef's Swiss cheese salad _____ 38
Chocolate & biscoff marquise _____ 148
Chocolate & coconut fondants _____ 144
Chocolate mousse with candied ginger _____ 158
Chorizo & olive clafouti _____ 8
Cod with mustard & tomato _____ 92
Coffee & walnut cake _____ 148
Coffee panna cotta _____ 173
Colorful mini-brochettes _____ 46
Cottage pie with sweet potatoes _____ 102
Crab risotto _____ 93
Cream of coral lentil & pumpkin soup _____ 29
Cream of endive & smoked
duck breast soup _____ 27
Cream of mushroom, chestnut,
hazelnut & cheese soup _____ 33
Cream of pumpkin soup _____ 32
Cream of Stilton & bacon soup _____ 22
Creamy mushroom & walnut soup _____ 33
Crispy ravioli salad _____ 43
Curried lentil, bacon & egg salad _____ 36

E

Eggplant & basil rolls _____ 16
Eggplant fans with goat cheese _____ 136
Endive & creamy maroilles gratin _____ 75

F

Fennel & goat cheese salad _____ 41
Fig & pistachio tart _____ 180
Figs with almond cream _____ 150
Florentine prawn gratin _____ 74
Fromage blanc tart _____ 153

G

Goat cheese, mint & raisin cake _____ 131
Grilled mackerel fillets & avocado sauce _____ 89
Grilled vegetable lasagna _____ 127
Grilled vegetable & peanut salad _____ 47
Grilled vegetable sandwiches _____ 126

I

Italian-style stuffed sardines _____ 86

L

Leek & ham gratin _____ 66
Lemon tart _____ 164
Linzer Torte _____ 174

M

Mackerel with a white wine sauce _____ 89
Maxi zucchini pizza _____ 53
Mediterranean style spaghetti _____ 138
Mini cheese & tomato croque-monsieur
sandwiches _____ 16
Mini pineapple tarts _____ 147
Monkfish & lime stew _____ 83
Mushroom & smoked duck breast quiche _____ 61
Mushroom Stroganoff _____ 121
Mussels in a pot _____ 78
Mussels in coconut milk _____ 81

182

N

Nutella fondant tart _____ 170

O

Onion & goat cheese tart _____ 50

P

Pappardelle with arugula & orange sauce __ 137
Peach melba _____ 164
Pear & almond cream spring rolls _____ 178
Pear & gingerbread tart _____ 156
Pear & verbena delight _____ 167
Pear & walnut crumble _____ 155
Peking duck & sauerkraut _____ 117
Plate of veal with caramelized carrots ___ 105
Pork & chorizo shish kebabs with sage ___ 110
Pork colombo with vegetables _____ 113
Pork tenderloin with chorizo _____ 106
Potato & mushroom gratin _____ 68
Potato salad _____ 42
Prune custard flan with salted butter ___ 169

R

Red berry crumble _____ 163
Risotto verde with mascarpone _____ 133
Roast leg of lamb with
pistachios & soft apricots_____ 100
Roquefort cheese omelet _____ 140

S

Salmon & cilantro pies _____ 54
Salmon, celery & chorizo potato pie ___ 85
Sautéed asparagus in balsamic vinegar __ 129
Sautéed prawns with mango juice ___ 95
Savory corn & smoked duck breast cake ___ 14
Spaghetti with queen scallops,
garlic flakes & pecorino cheese _____ 90
Spaghetti with tomato & chili pepper ___ 124

Spicy meatball shish kebabs with
carrot & cumin salad _____ 102
Spicy strawberry rice pudding _____ 176
Spinach & goat cheese calzone _____ 58
Split pea soup _____ 27
Spring vegetable tart _____ 56
Strawberry & mint tartlets _____ 176
Stuffed chicken surprise _____ 98
Sweet & sour lamb shanks with garlic ___ 114

T

Tandoori rack of lamb _____ 108
Thai cream of prawn soup _____ 24
Traditional macaroni gratin _____ 71

W

Walnut tart _____ 154
Warm bulgur & smoked chicken salad ___ 38
Whiting fillets baked in sea salt ___ 84

Z

Zucchini & feta cake _____ 122
Zucchini rolls with goat cheese _____ 19
Zucchini, chicken & Parmesan salad ___ 11

Photographic credits

Christine Fleurent (p. 63, 130); Valery Guedes (p. 10, 17, 43, 44, 55, 70, 72, 79, 85, 91, 99, 111, 116, 128, 139, 146, 176, 179); Valérie Lhomme (p. 15, 151); Catherine Madani (p. 18, 31, 93, 127, 160, 166, 169, 175); Jean-François Mallet (p. 25, 36, 152); Virginie Martin (p. 12); Alain Muriot (p. 45); Loïc Nicoloso (p. 51, 52, 56, 67, 28, 88, 94, 101, 132, 172, 181); Amélie Roche (p. 29, 69); Laurent Rouvrais (p. 26, 30, 39, 40, 60, 103, 104, 109, 125, 134, 155, 161, 165, 171); Pierre-Louis Viel (p. 8, 23, 59, 73, 80, 87, 107, 112, 115, 120, 123, 135, 141, 145, 149, 157); Bernard Winckelmann (p. 159).

Recipe credits

Solveig Darrigo (p. 29, 31, 82, 127, 166); Valery Drouet (p. 91, 112, 115); Eric Frechon (p. 69, 94, 160); Coco Jobard (p. 159); Irène Karsenty (p. 26, 30, 39, 40, 60, 72, 85, 88, 101, 104, 123, 132, 155, 161); Irène Karsenty and Pascale Mosnier (p. 25); Marie Leteuré (p. 15, 51, 52, 56, 67, 130, 151, 172, 181); Catherine Madani (p. 12, 18, 103, 125, 134, 171); Corinne Morin (p. 87); Pascale Mosnier (p. 8, 10, 17, 23, 43, 44, 45, 55, 59, 63, 70, 73, 79, 80, 93, 99, 107, 111, 116, 120, 128, 135, 139, 141, 145, 146, 149, 152, 157, 169, 175, 177, 179) and Karine Valentin for her advice on wines.

Contents and illustrations

Fotolia/Aleksandra Novakovic; Fotolia/ivaleksa.

Copyright © 2015, Marie Claire Publishing – Société d'Information et de Créations – SIC

Whitecap Books
First edition published 2015

MARIE CLAIRE EDITION CONTRIBUTORS:
Publishing director: Thierry Lamarre
Senior Editor: Adeline Lobut
Text and adaptation of the recipes: Catherine Gerbod
Iconographic research: Sylvie Creusy
Proofreading: Sophie Prétot, Isabelle Misery
Graphic design and layout: Either Studio

WHITECAP BOOKS EDITION CONTRIBUTORS:
Translation: Susan Allen Maurin
Editor: Claire Philipson
Typesetting: Robert Ondzik
Proofreading: Sonnet Force
Cover design: Andrew Bagatella

Printed in Romania

Data available from Library and Archives Canada

21 20 19 18 17 16 15   1 2 3 4 5 6 7

We acknowledge the financial support of the Government of Canada and the Province of British Columbia through the Book Publishing Tax Credit. Nous reconnaissons l'appui financier du gouvernement du Canada et la province de la Colombie-Britannique par le Book Publishing Tax Credit.